Princeton Theological Monograph Series

Dikran Y. Hadidian

General Editor

22

THE WILL OF GOD AND THE CROSS

Ron Morris

JONATHAN H. RAINBOW

The
Will Of God
And The Cross

An Historical and Theological Study of
John Calvin's Doctrine of
Limited Redemption

PICKWICK PUBLICATIONS
ALLISON PARK, PENNSYLVANIA

Published by Pickwick Publications
4137 Timberlane Drive
Allison Park, PA 15101-2932

Printed in the United States of America

Library of Congress Cataloging-in-Publications Data

Rainbow, Jonathan Herbold.
    The will of God and the cross : an historical and theological
study of John Calvin's doctrine of limited redemption / Jonathan
H. Rainbow.
      p. cm. -- (Princeton theological monograph series ; 22)
    Includes bibliographical references.
    ISBN 1-55635-005-8
    1. Predestination--History of doctrines--16th century. 2. Calvin,
Jean, 1506-1564--Contributions to doctrine of limited atonement.
3. Redemption--History of doctrines--16th century.   I. Title.
II. Series.
BT809.R35   1990
234'.9'092--dc20   90-30695
                                              CIP

To Pat

my partner in life

in redemption

and in writing about redemption

CONTENTS

PREFACE

The final shape of a work of historical research seldom reflects the strange and unexpected circumstances of its birth and formation. Historians are like detectives, working from clues, expecting to be led down one path but forced into others, never in control of the evidence but (if they are good historians!) controlled by it.

I do not mind admitting, therefore, that my interest in Calvin's theology of the extent of redemption was aroused while I was pursuing a completely different line of research. At one time during my doctoral studies I fully intended to write my dissertation on the revolutionary Anabaptist kingdom of Münster of 1534-35. During the process of collecting and surveying original and secondary sources on Münster I was inevitably exposed to the writings of Bernhard Rothmann, the Münster theologian; I noted with curiosity how Rothmann in several places emphasized that the Münster Anabaptists believed that Christ's death was intended for each and every human being. He did this, not casually, but polemically, as if there were someone out there saying the opposite, someone against whom the doctrine of universal redemption had to be defended.

I say that I noted this with curiosity, because I was at the time under the influence of what I call in this book the "Amyraut thesis," the view that the doctrine of limited redemption was not introduced into Protestant theology until much later in the 16th century, by Theodore Beza. So I wondered: who was teaching limited redemption in the 1530s? A brief search led to Martin Bucer. Then I wondered: is it possible, given the close personal and theological connections between Bucer and Calvin, that they held radically different doctrines of something as central as the death of Christ? This led to a reevaluation of Calvin's theology. and I wondered also: Is there some tradition preceding Bucer? This question led to a survey of medieval theology that led finally back to Augustine.

So the Anabaptist Bernhard Rothmann, who in the final orderly scheme that I have imposed on the material to shape it into a book is a very minor figure, mentioned only in passing, was actually the one who gave me my topic. I want to acknowledge his help.

Acknowledgment and gratitude must also go to many people whose conscientious work contributed to the writing of this book. I am grateful to the professionals of the Interlibrary Loan Department of the UCSB Library, who ransacked the libraries of America and Europe to find the materials I needed; to Profs. Jeffrey Russell and J. Sears McGee for constructively critical readings of my work as it progressed; to Prof. Dr. Peter Manns, Dr. Rolf Decot, and Dr. Markus Wriedt of the Institut für Europäische Geschichte for their encouragement to me during the writing of my dissertation and their patience with my German; to the Protestant Seminary of Strasbourg for access to early edition of Bucer's works; to Dr. Richard Muller of Fuller Theological Seminary, for his careful reading of my work and his helpful comments; and to my doctoral advisor, Abraham Friesen of UCSB, with whom I first read Calvin's Institutes as an undergraduate, and who was somehow able, while supervising me and guiding me, to treat me as a grown-up and a friend. Thanks, Abe.

Working with Dikran and Jean Hadidian of Pickwick Publications has been a delightful experience, for which I am also grateful.

I dedicate this book to my wife, Pat, for all she has done to see me through the labor of which this book is the most tangible fruit. The challenge of my going back to school, and then to West Germany for a year, with three small children, was one which she met victoriously, so much so that those years will always be for us a golden time.

Jonathan Rainbow
Porterville, California
January, 1990

1

AMYRAUT'S THESIS

Moyse Amyraut, professor of theology in the French Reformed academy of Saumur, said something that troubled the Reformed churches of the mid-seventeenth century: Christ, he insisted, died for each and every human being.

The question of whom Christ died for was not a new issue for Reformed theology. By Amyraut's day the Reformed creeds, preeminently the Canons of Dordt (1619) and the Westminster Standards (1647), had affirmed, as over against Roman Catholicism, Lutheranism, and the Dutch Remonstrants (or Arminians), that Christ died only for the predestined, or elect. But when Amyraut maintained the death of Christ for every single human being, he did so in a way that posed a new challenge to Reformed theology.

Defining the crucial terms

Before describing the precise nature of Amyraut's argument, we must define some of the basic terminology that will be used throughout this study. English speaking theologians often describe the view that Christ died for every human being as "universal atonement," and the view that he died only for the elect as "limited atonement." The term *atonement*, however, is peculiarly English, for which reason I prefer and will consistently use the term *redemption*, which in its Latin form *redemptio* is one of several words (Calvin used *expiatio*, *satisfactio*, and *reconciliatio* also) used by virtually all the theologians we will be examining, from Augustine to Calvin, to denote the meaning of the death of Christ. If what took place, then, in the death of Christ was redemption, the question is: was this redemption achieved for every person or only for the elect? In this study I will refer to those who maintained that Christ died for every person as *universal redemptionists*, and to those who maintained that he died only for the elect as *limited redemptionists*.

It should be emphasized also that universal redemptionists, except where otherwise indicated, did not maintain that every human being will be ultimately saved. Universal redemption, in other words, did not imply *universal salvation*. The doctrine of universal salvation is sometimes known as the doctrine of *apokatastasis*, or simply *universalism*. It should not be confused with the doctrine of universal redemption as we encounter it throughout this study.

Amyraut's argument

Moyse Amyraut (1596-1664) taught divine predestination just as Reformed theology had come to define it; he also taught that Christ died for every human being. This concatenation of particular election and universal redemption was a new problem for the Reformed; it was not the frontal assault on particularism to which they had become accustomed, but neither was it orthodoxy as defined by the Reformed confessions, especially the definitive ones of the seventeenth century, the Canons of Dordt (1619) and the Westminster Confession (1647). An alternative kind of "Reformed" theology had appeared.

Amyraut's theology precipitated a new period of intramural debate within Reformed theology about the extent of Christ's redemption. It was, above all, a theological and biblical issue to be settled. But Amyraut also made a disconcerting historical claim. He claimed that his understanding of the extent of redemption was in fact that of the "father" of Reformed theology, John Calvin himself. He claimed that Calvin had taught universal redemption, and that the doctrine of limited redemption was actually the construct of Theodore Beza (1519-1605), Calvin's protegé and successor as the leading theologian of Geneva. Thus, in Amyraut, a distinctive view of Reformed history emerged: that the purity of the Reformed gospel, as taught and preached by Calvin, had been seriously compromised by Beza, that the Reformed churches had in the meantime followed Beza, and that Amyraut's own theology, with its doctrine of universal redemption, was in fact the recovery of genuine and original "Calvinism."[1] Reformed theology, through its consolidation in the seventeenth century, had comfortably assumed John Calvin as its founding father. Now Amyraut was saying that the great Reformed confessions, Dordt and Westminster, which held limited redemption, were not really "Calvinistic" at all.

Amyraut did not go unchallenged. His doctrine of universal redemption was set upon by the orthodox Reformed establishment, including defenders of the orthodox position such as André Rivet, Frederick Spanheim, and, most importantly, Pierre du Moulin.[2] These contestants also took issue with Amyraut's thesis about Calvin and Reformed history. The lines were drawn: one side claimed Calvin for universal redemption, the other for limited redemption, and both sides appealed to evidence from Calvin's own writings for proof.

The theological question is clearly an important one. But it is the historical question that concerns us here. Is the "Amyraut thesis" (that Calvin held universal redemption) correct? What did John Calvin really believe and teach about the extent of Christ's redemption?

Amyraut and the scholars

This question has become a contemporary one as scholars have given attention to seventeenth-century Reformed theology,

---

[1] Amyraut's interpretation of Calvin is found in **Defense de la doctrine de Calvin sur le sujet e'Election et de la Reprobation** (Saumur: Desbordes, 1644); **Brief Traité de la Predestination. Avec l'Eschantillon de la doctrine de Calvin sur le mesme suiet** (Saumur: Desbordes, 1658); **Fidei Mosis Amyraldi circa errores Arminianorum declaratio** (Saumur: Lesnier, 1646). For a complete Amyraut bibliography see Roger Nicole, **Moyse Amyraut. A Bibliography with special reference to the controversy on universal grace** (New York, London: Garland Publishers, 1981).

[2] Cf. André Rivet, **Andreae Riveti . . . synopsis doctrinae de natura ert gratia. Excerpta ex Mosis Amyraldi . . . tractatu de praedestinatione . . .** (Amsterdam, 1649); Frederick Spanheim, **Disputatio de gratia universali** (Leyden, 1644); Pierre du Moulin, **De Mosis Amyraldi adversus Fridericum Spanheimium libro judicium** (Rotterdam, 1649); **Esclaircissement des controverses Salmuriennes** (Leyden, 1648).

and to Amyraut in particular. Amyraut's claim has sent theologians and historians back to Calvin, and various answers have emerged. Some have concluded that a firm judgment about Calvin's doctrine of the extent of redemption is not possible. Others--Louis Goumaz, John Murray, J. I. Packer, Ian McPhee, and Paul Helm, who wrote a monograph entitled **Calvin and the Calvinists** (1982),[1] to date the most thorough attempt at rebutting the Amyraut thesis--have concluded that Amyraut was wrong about Calvin. But the predominant viewpoint in the recent scholarly discussions has been the view of Amyraut, the "Amyraut thesis," that Calvin was an advocate of universal redemption.

This interpretation of Calvin has sometimes emerged in connection with the study of what has come to be called "Reformed scholasticism," which is also in its way a revival of the historical critique offered by Amyraut. In the view of scholars like H. E. Weber, Ernst Bizer, Walter Kickel, Basil Hall, and David Steinmetz[2], the phenomenon of "Reformed scholasticism" was the hardening and rationalizing of Reformed theology which began to occur after Calvin's departure from the scene. According to this interpretation, there was, under the leadership of Beza, a

---

[1] Louis Goumaz, **La doctrine de salut (doctrina salutis) d'après le commentaires de Calvin sur le Nouveau Testament** (Lyon, 1907). John Murray, review of Paul van Buren's **Christ in our Place, Banner of Truth** 234 (March 1983): 20-22. J. I. Packer; *Calvin the Theologian,* in **John Calvin: A Collection of Essays,** ed. G. Duffield (Grand Rapids: Wm. B. Eerdmans Publishing Co., 1966), p. 151. Ian McPhee, *Conserver or Transformer of Calvin's Thought? A Study of the Origins and development of Theodore Beza's Thought 1550-70* (Ph.D. dissertation, Cambridge, 1979). Paul Helm, *Calvin, English Calvinism, and the logic of doctrinal development,* **Scottish Journal of Theology** 34, No. 2 (1981): 179-85; **Calvin and the Calvinists** (Edinburgh: Banner of Truth, 1982).

[2] Basil Hall, *Calvin against the Calvinists,* Duffield. Walter Kickel, **Vernunft und Offenbarung bei Theodor Beza** (Neukirchen, 1967). Ernst Bizer, **Frühorthodoxie und Rationalismus** (Zurich, 1963). Hans Emil Weber, **Reformation, Orthodoxie, und Rationalismus, Beiträge zur Förderung Christlicher Theologie,** vols. 37, 51 (Gütersloh, 1937, 1951). David Steinmetz, **Reformers in the Wings** (Philadelphia: Fortress Press, 1971), p. 167.

discernable shift away from the biblical-humanistic theological method of Calvin to one governed by an Aristotelian-deductive epistemology. In Reformed theology, so reconceived, the doctrine of predestination became the logical starting point for the whole system. Some scholars of "Reformed scholasticism" assert that the doctrine of limited redemption was one of the results of this new method. Again, and in a roundabout way, the Amyraut thesis concerning Calvin and Reformed history has been revived. Amyraut was a much harassed man in his time; perhaps he has begun to have his posthumous revenge three centuries later, for his interpretation of Calvin has come to be shared by the majority of historians who study such things.[1]

The most important recent statements of the Amyraut thesis were in books by François Laplanche, Brian Armstrong, and R. T. Kendall. Laplanche's 1965 study was the pioneering modern investigation of Amyraut.[2] In the process of setting out the theology of Amyraut, Laplanche had numerous opportunities to comment on the doctrine of redemption, and he concurred with Amyraut that Calvin held universal redemption.[3]

The tendency to appraise Calvin through the eyes of Amyraut was continued by Brian Armstrong in a 1969 study which centered, like Laplanche's, on Amyraut, but which also dealt extensively with

---

[1] A recent, very refreshing exception to the predominant trend in recent scholarship was Richard Muller, **Christ and the Decree: Christology and Predestination in Reformed Theology from Calvin to Perkins** (Grand Rapids: Baker Book House, 1988). Muller argued convincingly that Reformed theology after Calvin, while often organized differently, was the same in substance as Calvin's. Muller also maintained that Calvin held limited redemption.

[2] François Laplanche, **Orthodoxie et Prédication. L'Oeuvre d'Amyraut et la querelle de la grâce universelle** (Paris: Presses Universitaires de France, 1965). Laplanche's work was actually preceded by the doctoral dissertation of Jürgen Moltmann, *Gnadenbund und Gnadenwahl: Die Prädestinationslehre des Moyse Amyraut, dargestellt im Zusammenhang der heilsgeschichtlich-foederaltheologie Tradition der Akademie von Saumur* (Ph.D. dissertation, Göttingen, 1951).

[3] Laplanche, pp. 24, 115.

Amyraut's relationship to the entire Reformed tradition.[1]
Armstrong cast the struggle within the French Reformed Church
as one between a humanistically grounded Reformed tradition
(Calvin, Amyraut) and Reformed scholasticism (Beza, du Moulin).
He blamed Theodore Beza for engineering a major departure from
Calvin; he attributed the "rigid teaching" of limited redemption to
Beza and saw it as a necessary deduction from Beza's
supralapsarianism and Aristotelianism[2], and he agreed with
Amyraut that Calvin held universal redemption. He cited in a
lengthy footnote several Calvin texts to prove this last point.
Amyraut, he concluded, was the real "Calvinist."

This thesis was also employed by R. T. Kendall with reference
to the English theological context, in **Calvin and English
Calvinism to 1649** (1979).[3] Kendall argued that English Calvinistic
theology followed the lead of Beza and other "Reformed
scholastics" like Ursinus, Martyr, and Zanchius rather than that of
Calvin; to be specific, it lost Calvin's doctrine of saving faith and
got mired in the problem of Christian assurance. Kendall
attributed this directly to the introduction of the doctrine of
limited redemption. According to him, Calvin's doctrine of
assurance as the essence of faith was rooted in the doctrine of
universal redemption, and with the introduction of the Bezan
doctrine, the focus of assurance shifted away from Christ to the
subjective spiritual condition of the believer and thus made
assurance to rest on shifting sand. Because Kendall's whole thesis
thus rested on the alleged theological chasm between Calvin and
Beza, his exposition of Calvin's theology was much fuller--and, one
must say, much more basic to the validity of his thesis--than those

---

[1] Brian Armstrong, **Calvinism and the Amyraut Heresy: Protestant
Scholasticism and Humanism in Seventeenth Century France** (Madison:
The University of Wisconsin Press, 1969).

[2] Armstrong, pp. 41-42.

[3] R. T. Kendall, **Calvin and English Calvinism to 1649** (Oxford: The
University Press, 1979). Mention might also be made of John Bray,
Theodore Beza's Doctrine of Predestination (Nieuwkoop: B. de Graaf,
1975). Bray was clearly dependent on Armstrong for his evaluation of
Calvin's doctrine of redemption.

of Laplanche and Armstrong.

In Kendall's analysis, Calvin emerged in the image of Amyraut, as a theologian who taught both particular election and universal redemption. Christ's death was not the effectuation of the decree of election for Calvin, said Kendall--if it were, of course, it would be limited, like election, to the elect portion of the human race[1]--rather, the effectuation of election was achieved by Christ's intercession at the right hand of God: "What Calvin does not do is to link the scope of Christ's intercessory prayer to Christ's death, as those after him tended to do."[2] Christ's death, in Kendall's analysis of Calvin, was universal, but his intercession is only for the elect. Because of universal redemption, said Kendall, Calvin's doctrine of assurance was Christocentric, while for his successors it became introspective and anthropocentric. "It must therefore be argued that, as a result of this soteriological position [limited redemption] Beza's doctrine inhibits the believer from looking directly to Christ's death for assurance."[3] Kendall also attempted to distance Calvin's exegesis of the relevant biblical texts from that of the Bezan tradition: Calvin, he said, never resorted to the device of interpreting the terms "all" and "world" in a less than universalistic way, as those after him did.[4] Kendall recognized that the use of such hermeneutical devices would fundamentally change the manner in which Calvin's universalistic language should be understood.

Kendall's book was generally received as a major contribution

---

[1] "The decree of election, however, is not rendered effectual by the death of Christ. For if that were true, it follows that (1) Christ obviously did not die for the whole world after all, or (2) since he died for all, all are elected." Kendall, p. 15. Kendall was working backwards from the assumption that Calvin believed in universal redemption to the conclusion that therefore the death of Christ cannot have carried out the decree of election. This is impeccable logic, but, as we shall see, the starting point is wrong.

[2] Kendall, pp. 14 (footnote 1), 17.

[3] Kendall, p. 29.

[4] "He [Calvin] generally leaves verses like this alone, but never does he explain, for example, that 'all' does not mean *all* or that 'world' does not mean *world*, as those after him tended to do." Kendall, p. 13, footnote 2.

to the history of Calvinist history and theology. It is to date the most ambitious modern defense of the Amyraut thesis.

The flaws of the Amyraut thesis

But the Amyraut thesis is seriously flawed. For one thing, its proponents have depended almost exclusively on a prooftext method which consists largely of extracting various statements of Calvin to the effect that Christ died for the "world" or for "all," and insisting that these prove the case. It should be said too that those who have recently written against the Amyraut thesis have tended to do the same thing. Neither viewpoint has adequately addressed the evidence presented by the other. Conspicuous by its absence so far is any systematic treatment of Calvin's thought on the extent of redemption from the inside of his whole theology, in relationship to its dominant themes, including an analysis of both the universalistic statements and those that qualify them. It is one of my goals to provide such a treatment in this book. Calvin's doctrine of the death of Christ deserves to be lifted from polemics; Calvin deserves to speak for himself, and at length.

The Amyraut thesis has also been flawed by a fundamentally unhistorical approach. The scholars have come at Calvin backwards, through events and theologies which came after he was dead and gone, whether "Reformed scholasticism" (Steinmetz, Bray), Amyraut (Laplanche, Armstrong), or Puritanism (Kendall). Calvin has been repeatedly interpreted through the lense of some later development. It is obvious that Calvin cannot have been influenced by these things. Consequently, there is a need to set Calvin in his own historical-theological context, in the stream which flowed to him from the past, and to place him methodologically at the *end* of the history of the doctrine rather than at its beginning. To be blunt, there is a need to get Amyraut out of the picture.

The proponents of the Amyraut thesis take little account at all of the history that preceded Calvin; they are, it seems, unaware that Calvin the predestinarian theologian inherited a thousand-year tradition that taught limited redemption. It is a major goal of this book to identify that tradition and to show Calvin's relationship to it and dependence upon it.

2

AUGUSTINE: THE OMNIPOTENCE OF GOD AND THE DEATH OF CHRIST

Augustine of Hippo (d.430) is well known as a defender of predestination. What is not often noted is that Augustine's doctrine of double predestination, forged in his controversies with the Pelagians, had as its less conspicuous sibling the doctrine of limited redemption.[1]

The omnipotence of God

The granite foundation of Augustine's mature soteriology was the omnipotence of God. The Apostles' Creed itself, he noted, begins with the declaration of the divine omnipotence: "I believe in God the Father Almighty, maker of heaven and earth."[2] The act of *creatio ex nihilo* provides the pattern for all that God does.

Augustine, of course, was not alone in asserting the divine omnipotence; it was part of the common stock of Christian theology. Even Augustine's Pelagian opponents would have agreed in principle that God is omnipotent. It is how Augustine interpreted God's omnipotence which was decisive for his

---

[1] On Augustine's doctrine of predestination, see J.B. Mozley, **A Treatise on the Augustinian Doctrine of Predestination** (London, 1855). A standard history of atonement theory is R.S. Franks, **The Work of Christ** (London and New York, 1962). It is occasionally still asserted that Augustine did not teach double predestination (e.g. Larry Sharp, *The Doctrines of Grace in Calvin and Augustine*, **Evangelical Quarterly** 52 (1980):89), but in our judgment double predestination was clearly his mature view.

[2] **Contra secundam Juliani responsionem opus imperfectum**, Migne, **Patrologiae cursus completus, Series Latina** 45:1072. (Migne after this cited as **MPL**.)

soteriology. The Pelagians, trying to make room for human freedom, saw divine power as a kind of limitless potentiality, rather like a powerful engine running at idle speed. In other words, they saw omnipotence as *capability*: God can do whatever he wills. On this basis it was possible for them to assert that God, although omnipotent, has by his own choice opted not to use the fullness of his power, has voluntarily relinquished a portion of the determination of events to the will of man. So it is possible for God to will something but for that which he wills not to come to pass.

For Augustine divine omnipotence was not mere capability; it was *effectuation*. God always and actually *does* what he wills. There is for God a perfect correspondence of will and act, of volition and effectuation. "The will of the Omnipotent is never defeated . . . God never wills anything which he does not perform."[1] The universe and human history, both on the grand and the minute scales, are the product of the putting forth of divine power according to the divine will. "Therefore nothing is done except the Omnipotent wills it to be done."[2] And genuine contingency--contingency on the same level of causation as the will of God--is eliminated. "The will of God is the necessity of things."[3]

It is likely that Augustine's understanding of God's omnipotence was, in part, a reaction against Manicheanism, to which he had once been attracted. The God of Mani was one whose power was severely limited by the existence of an equally aggressive and ultimate evil principle in the *kosmos*. Although the good God eventually conquers evil, the struggle is a close one, and the good God often appears passive while evil rages.[4] The God in whom Augustine, prodded by the Pelagians, came finally to believe is, by contrast, nothing if not active, a willing, acting, doing God in a monistic *kosmos*. The Manicheans were willing to have a less

---

[1] Enchiridion 102, **Corpus Christianorum, Series Latina** (after this cited as **CCSL**) 46:104.

[2] **Enchiridion 95, CCSL** 46:99.

[3] **Gen. ad litt. 6.15.26, MPL** 34:350.

[4] Peter Brown, **Augustine of Hippo: A Biography** (London, Boston: Faber & Faber, 1967), pp. 52, 394-5.

than omnipotent God in order to achieve a clean solution to the problem of God's association with evil; Augustine was willing to face this problem, or at least to leave it in mystery, for the sake of a truly omnipotent God.

This was supremely important to Augustine because the omnipotent God who creates out of nothing was the *sine qua non* of his doctrine of grace. For grace, like omnipotence, can be understood as a kind of potentiality. For the Pelagian, grace was God's willingness to save fallen humans; God has gone to great and even sacrificial lengths to reveal this willingness to mankind; but all of God's willingness does not, in and of itself, save a single human being. God may will to save and yet not save, if the will of man intervenes against the will of God. For Augustine, however, grace was not simply God's will to save but also the omnipotent effectuation of that will. Grace was quite simply, for Augustine, the salvation of fallen human beings. And this was so because grace, like all of God's decisions, is omnipotent and therefore irresistibly effectual. When God wills to save, he saves.

Limited redemption

The omnipotence of God was the presupposition of Augustine's doctrine of redemption. The death of Christ, as an omnipotent act of divine grace and divine will for the salvation of men, is irresistibly effectual. Whom God wills to save through the death of Christ, he does in fact save, and so the intent of Christ's sacrifice can be measured by the result. Since not all men are finally saved, it must be that Christ did not intend by his death to save all men, but only those whom he actually saves, that is the predestined. So ran Augustine's theological thinking about the death of Christ.

The limitation of redemption to the elect appeared occasionally in Augustine in contexts where the doctrine of Christ's death was not the principal topic. In one sense, such offhand remarks are a more revealing witness to his belief in limited redemption than are the longer texts which will be examined shortly, because they show that this belief was a deeply held assumption capable of being called into service without much provocation. For example:

> What did he mean, then, in saying to them [the unbelieving Jews],
> "You are not of my sheep"? That he saw them predestined to
> everlasting destruction, not won to eternal life by the price of his
> own blood.[1]

The apposition of the phrases *ad sempiternam interitum
praedestinatos* and *non ad vitam aeternam sui sanguinis pretio
comparatos* was theologically significant; it showed that in
Augustine's mind predestination to destruction and not having
been won to eternal life by the blood of Christ were parallel
concepts, for both concepts described those who are not "sheep."
And the sheep in this context were the elect. In a similar remark,
Augustine asked his listening congregation:

> And why is it that you have thus willingly listened to Christ in me?
> Because you are the sheep of Christ, purchased with the blood of
> Christ . . . He and only he was the purchaser, who shed precious
> blood, the precious blood of him who was without sin. Yet he also
> made precious the blood of his own [people], for whom he paid
> the price of his own blood.[2]

This passage was pervaded by the assumption that the blood of
Christ is a special gift of Christ to the sheep.

For Augustine, the death of Christ did not accomplish the
mere possibility of salvation, but actually saved those for whom it
was intended.

> Through this Mediator God makes known that he makes those
> whom he has redeemed from evil by his blood, everlastingly
> good.[3]

The kingdom which Christ now gathers, and which will constitute
the final number of the redeemed, is composed of those whom he
has redeemed with his blood, and, by clear implication, not others:

---

[1] CCSL 36:415.
[2] CCSL 36:404.
[3] De correptione et gratia 30, MPL 44:935.

"First Christ, then those who are Christ's at his coming; then the end, when he delivers over the kingdom to the God and Father"[I Cor. 15:23,24], that is, those whom he has redeemed with his own blood, he will also deliver over to the contemplation of his own Father.[1]

This limitation of Christ's death to the predestined was not for Augustine a simple deduction from the doctrine of predestination. As would appear in the cases of Thomas Aquinas and Amyraut, it was not the case in the history of Christian theology that a belief in predestination automatically brought in its wake the limitation of Christ's death to the elect. For Augustine the deeper principle was the divine omnipotence, and from this principle flowed both the doctrines of predestination and of limited redemption. Since the divine will is the wellspring of salvation, and since both predestination and redemption are acts of the divine will, they must come to fruition. Predestination and limited redemption are not, therefore, related as parent and child, but as siblings.

The "all" and "world" texts
      Augustine's Pelagian opponents, even the brilliant Julian of Eclanum, seem not to have made much use of the New Testament statements that Christ died for "all" and for the "world." So Augustine was never challenged hard on this point, as some of his later followers would be. Still, when he came to such texts in the course of exposition, he was careful to explain them in ways that limited Christ's redemption to the elect. For the limited redemptionist, these texts force the question: if "all" and "world" do not mean *every* human being, what do they mean?
      One such text is Colossians 1:20, which states that Christ, by his blood, reconciled "all things, whether things in earth or things in heaven" to God. In Augustine's interpretation of the passage, "all things" described the church triumphant in its eschatological totality, inclusive of both redeemed men and the holy angels. Its

[1] CCSL 36:498.

human portion is composed exclusively of the predestined, whose number corresponds exactly to that of the fallen angels.

> The things which are on earth are gathered when those who are predestined to eternal life are redeemed from their old corruption. And thus, through that single sacrifice . . . heavenly things are brought into peace with earthly things and earthly things with heavenly.

The purpose of the death of Christ is therefore the reconciliation of the predestined to God and to the angelic host. "All things" does not mean every human being.[1]

Another important verse for Augustine was II Corinthians 5:19, which states that "God was in Christ, reconciling the world to himself." We find Augustine's interpretation of the term "world," as used here, in the context of his exposition of another passage, John 17. There are, he explained, two meanings of "world." On the one hand, it can refer to the world of the reprobate, as it does when Jesus says, "I pray not for the world" (John 17:9). It can, on the other hand, refer to the world of the elect, the world which has been predestined to salvation.

> There is a world of which it is written, "For the Son of man came not to condemn the world, but that the world through him might be saved," and also where the apostle says, "God was in Christ, reconciling the world to himself."[2]

The world of the predestined is the object of Christ's reconciling work. The quotation above shows that this was Augustine's understanding, not only of II Cor. 5:19, but also of the famous text in John 3:16-17.

The double signification of "world" also underlay Augustine's understanding of I John 2:2: "And he is the propitiation for our sins, and not for ours only, but for the whole world." One could

---

[1] Enchiridion 61-2, CCSL 46:82.

[2] Trac. in Joh. CX, CCSL 36:622-3. The concept of two worlds, one of the elect and the other of the reprobate, appeared also in Augustine's treatment of John 12:31, CCSL 36:450.

take this biblical affirmation as the clearest kind of statement of Christ's death for every individual, but Augustine did not.

> See, you have here the church throughout the whole world; do not follow false justifiers who are really cutters-off. Be in that mountain which has filled the whole earth, because "Christ is the propitiation for our sins; and not for ours only, but also the sins of the whole world," which he has bought with his blood.[1]

Augustine was using the universality implicit in the verse to emphasize the catholicity of the church; the "false cutters-off" were heretics and schismatics who lead people away from the one true church. But it is also clear that the "whole world" *was* for Augustine the church itself. Drawing on the Old Testament image of Daniel's fifth kingdom ("But the stone which shattered the image became a great mountain and filled the whole earth," Daniel 2:35), Augustine referred to the catholic church as this mountain. It is also the whole world which Christ has bought with his blood. That he had in mind here the world of the predestined, after the manner of his exegesis of John 17:9 and II Cor. 5:19, appears from yet another comment on I John 2:2:

> Therefore, the whole world [of I John 2:2] is the church, and the whole world hates the church. Therefore the world hates the world.

Two worlds oppose each other; the one is the beneficiary of Christ's propitiatory work, while the other remains implacably hostile to Christ and the church. And, lest this begin to sound like some kind of ultimate dualism, Augustine went on to explain that the redeemed world is taken *from* the other, that it too was once "inimical, damned, and contaminated," but that it, and it only, has been reconciled, forgiven, and saved.[2] Thus the duality of the two worlds is not ontological but redemptive. There is a redeemed world only by the will of God, because he has chosen to redeem

---

[1] In Epistolam Joannis ad Parthos, Trac. I, MPL 35:1984.
[2] CCSL 36:544.

a portion of the fallen world. And for this study the important point is that, for Augustine, the world which Christ redeemed with his death was the world of the elect.

In John 12:32 Augustine confronted the words of Christ, "And I, if I am lifted up, will draw all things to myself." Since "lifting up" is in the context a metaphor for Christ's crucifixion, the verse amounts to a statement that Christ will die for "all things." There is a textual ambiguity here of which Augustine was aware: the Greek texts say both "all things" (*panta*) and "all men" (*pantas*), which showed up in the Old Latin as *omnia* and *omnes*. Augustine offered interpretations to cover both options. As to *omnia*, which he preferred, he said that it refers to the various parts of the human person--spirit, soul, and body. In this case the meaning of Jesus' words would be that Christ by his death redeems the whole human person. Then, perhaps sensing that this was a bit strained, he offered a second and more substantial interpretation based on the assumption that *omnia* means human beings:

> Or, if by "all things" it is men that are to be understood, we can speak of all things that are predestined to salvation, of which all he declared, when previously speaking of his sheep, that not one of them would be lost. And surely all classes of men, both of every language and every age, and all grades of rank, and all diversities of talents, and all the professions of lawful and useful arts, and all else that can be named according to the innumerable differences by which men, except in sin alone, are separated from each other, from the highest to the lowest and from the king to the beggar, "all," he says, "will I draw after me."[1]

In no case, then, did Augustine interpet the passage to mean that Christ draws *every* man to himself in his death. The universalism implicit in the word "all" is a universalism of *kinds* of men, not of *individual* men. Predestined individuals are drawn to Christ in his death from every category of human beings. This "universalism of kinds" (my label) was for Augustine, and would become for those who followed him in the limited redemptionist tradition, an

[1] CCSL 36:450.

enormously important interpretive idea. For it meets two needs: firstly, it preserves the particularity of God's saving will and action toward the elect; secondly, it seeks to do justice to the obvious universality of the passages in question. To put this negatively: Augustine's exegesis could neither posit that Christ died for every human being nor could it pretend that the word "all" does not exist. It is important to note that this method of exegesis would be completely unnecessary if Augustine had been a universal redemptionist. So the use of this concept of the universalism of kinds to interpret the biblical words "all" and "world" became, with Augustine, one of the characteristic features of the limited redemptionist position.

Above all others, the text I Timothy 2:4 was a wedge which parted universal redemptionists from limited redemptionists: "[God] wills all men to be saved and come to the knowledge of the truth." Even by Augustine's time this text had had a history of interpretation.[1] Origen, operating on the supposition that what God wills does in fact happen, had used it to support his doctrine of *apokatastasis*, or universal salvation.[2] John Chrysostom, himself not a believer in universal salvation, took a different direction with the passage. He posed the logical conundrum: if God wills all men to be saved, why are all men not saved? To answer this he introduced the distinction, later taken over by Thomas Aquinas,

---

[1] Cf. J. Turmel, *Histoire de l'Interpretation de I Tim. II,4*, **Revue d'histoire et de litterature religieuses** 5 (1900): 385-415. Turmel gave a survey of the interpretation of the verse from its earliest mention in the patristic literature (Pseudo-Justin) to St. Thomas and some later Thomists. There was no treatment, however, of any Protestant theologians.

[2] In an obvious sense Origen and Augustine were far apart: Origen believed in universal salvation and Augustine did not. In another sense, however, they must be ranged together against someone like Chrysostom, because for both Origen and Augustine the will of God expressed in I Tim. 2:4 is an effectual will. What God wills is what happens. Several centuries later the Augustinian, Gottschalk of Orbais, would prefer the universalism of Origen to the conditional grace of his opponents, since at least in Origen's system the blood of Christ does not go to waste. Cf. J. Pelikan, **The Christian Tradition: A History of the Development of Doctrine**, 4 vols. (Chicago and London, Univ. of Chicago Press, 1971-), 3:92.

between the antecedent and consequent wills of God. Antecedently, God wills the salvation of all, but this will depends on the fulfillment of a further condition. The consequent will of God is the statement of the condition: God wills that all who believe the gospel be saved. Many whom God wills to be saved by his antecedent will are not actually saved because they do not fulfill the condition. This consequent (conditional) will of God is, according to Chrysostom, the will of which I Tim. 2:4 speaks.[1] Thus it is possible to say that God wills the salvation of all but that not all are saved. Problem solved.

But not for Augustine, whose exegesis followed neither Origen nor Chrysostom. Unlike Origen, he did not believe in universal salvation, and unlike Chrysostom, he did not believe that the will of God to save is ever ineffectual. His interpretation of I Tim. 2:4 was bounded by these considerations, and within them he offered two ways to understand the passage, both in **Enchiridion** 103. Although Augustine did not clearly distinguish them as alternate exegeses, they are, in fact, distinct, and we shall treat them as such.

The first approach, and that which was, judging by the space which Augustine alloted to it, dominant in his own mind, was the universalism of kinds which we have already observed in his treatment of John 12:32.

> We are to understand by "all men" the human race in all its varieties of rank and circumstance--kings, subjects . . . [the list goes on for several lines here], for which of all these classes is there out of which God does not will that men should be saved in all nations through his only-begotten Son our Lord?[2]

The key words are "out of which." God does not will to save through Christ all individual men, but rather individual men from all classes and kinds. Augustine also interpreted I Tim. 2:4 this way in **De correptione et gratia**.

---

[1] In Ephes. homil. I.2. In Migne, **Patrologiae cursus completus, Series Graeca** 62:13.

[2] **Enchiridion** 103, **CCSL** 46:105.

> "He wills all men to be saved" is so said that all the predestined
> are understood by it, because every kind of men is among them.[1]

Now the obvious objection to this approach is that it is pure
special pleading, that the word "all" transparently means *every*, and
that Augustine is doing violence to the text. But no, rejoined
Augustine. The equation of "all" and "every" is not as obvious as
it may seem. He produced some examples. The Pharisees, says
Jesus, tithe all (*omne*) herbs, but this cannot mean literally every
herb without exception, in which case it would mean that they had
travelled the whole world over to find every existing herb. Clearly
it refers to the limited range of herbs available in a certain place
and time. And when Paul says that he tries to please all men
(*omnibus*), this certainly cannot mean all men individually, since
it is clear that he did not please his enemies and persecutors.[2]
The term "all," Augustine was saying, is like most words
susceptible of a wide range of meaning, depending on context. To
insist from the outset that it must always mean "every" is
excessively rigid and would, if applied consistently, result in
numerous absurdities. In I Tim. 2:4, its meaning was conditioned
for Augustine both by the near context, in which Paul speaks of
kings and those in authority (that is, a particular kind of people),
and by the wider biblical-theological context, in which it is
apparent that the omnipotent God does not will ineffectually.
    There is still another way of construing the word "all," which
Augustine only touched on briefly in the **Enchiridion** but
expanded upon elsewhere. We may understand the statement that
God wills all men to be saved to mean that

> no man is saved unless God wills his salvation; not that there is
> no man whose salvation he does not will, but that no man is saved
> apart from his will.[3]

---

[1] **De correptione et gratia, MPL** 44:943.
[2] **De correptione et gratia, MPL** 44:943.
[3] **Enchiridion** 103, **CCSL** 46:104. Cf. also **MPL** 44:760.

In this interpretation, the emphasis falls not on the fact that God wills *all* to be saved, but that *God* wills all (i.e. any who are saved) to be saved. This somewhat abstruse concept came to life when Augustine provided some concrete illustrations. If we say, for example, "There is a midwife in the city of Hippo who delivers all (*omnes*)," it is clearly understood that the universal term *omnes* is limited to a specific category, namely, all new babies. Likewise, if we say, "There is in Hippo a teacher who teaches all," we mean, not that literally every person in Hippo is taught, but that those who are taught are taught by this one man. The midwife, in effect, has a monopoly on delivering babies and the teacher on teaching; she is the *only* midwife and he the *only* teacher. So, in I Tim. 2:4, the meaning is that God is the only Savior, the only one whose will effects the redemption of men. This is also the manner in which Augustine repeatedly handled the Adam-Christ parallel of Romans 5, which does not mean that the same number of men are redeemed through Christ as fell through Adam, but that all who fall do so only through Adam, and all who are saved are saved only through Christ.[1] This "exclusive universalism" would be found alongside the concept of "universalism of kinds" in the exegesis of those who followed Augustine.

In the final analysis, Augustine was less concerned about which interpretation of I Tim. 2:4 is finally adopted than he was to preserve the omnipotence of God. Any interpretation which leaves God ineffectually willing the salvation of men was for Augustine out of contention, and any interpretation which maintains God's sovereign will was acceptable.

> When we hear and read in the scripture that he "wills all men to be saved," although we know well that all men are not saved, we are not on that account to restrict the omnipotence of God . . . the Omnipotent cannot will in vain whatsoever he wills . . . And we may interpret it in any other way we please, as long as we are not forced to believe that the omnipotent God has willed anything

---

[1] **De peccatorum meritis et remissione, MPL** 44:141. This interpretation can also be seen in **MPL** 44:270-1, 119-20, and 45:1198

to be done which was not done.[1]

All exegetes have presuppositions that influence their conclusions; unlike most, Augustine laid his out on the table.

Although I Tim. 2:4 says nothing directly about redemption or the death of Christ, it is nevertheless a text which vitally affected the discussions of the extent of redemption. For to speak of God's will to save is certainly to say something about the redemptive work of Christ. This connection becomes explicit in the text itself, which goes on to say, "For there is one God, and one mediator between God and man, the man Christ Jesus, who gave himself a ransom for all" (I Tim. 2:5,6). Because the whole text, from v. 4 to v. 6, draws together the divine will to save all and the divine act of redemption for all, it became for both universal and limited redemptionists a *crux interpretationis*. This was the case throughout the medieval period and into the Reformation. No other text would come up so often in Calvin's discussions of predestination, and no other text would provide a better basis on which to understand both his own doctrine of redemption and his place in the Augustinian tradition.

Augustine bequeathed a problem to his successors in the middle ages: they all wanted to be "Augustinian," but very few of them wanted to believe that God did not really will the salvation of every human, had predestined some to life and some to damnation (what Isidore of Seville, writing some two hundred years later, would call "double predestination"[2]), and had sent Christ only for those predestined to eternal life. The problem with Augustine's doctrine of grace was, as J. Pelikan notes, that it was all too clear.[3]

This cluster of soteriological doctrines proved too difficult for the western church to swallow--not to mention the Greek east, with its much stronger stress on human freedom and self-determination. This statement must be understood as a generalization, for there was no monolithic Catholic position on

[1] **Enchiridion** 103, **CCSL** 46:104.
[2] **MPL** 83:606.
[3] J. Pelikan, 3:81.

the matter, much less any way to enforce it, and it was still possible for theologians to assert Augustine's soteriology as he had taught it. But on the whole Augustine's theology of grace underwent a modification which involved the muting or abandoning of what were considered its more objectionable features. And the theologians who continued, against the mainstream, to assert Augustine's doctrine of limited redemption tended to be men on the fringe, troublemakers, or even heretics.

3

LIMITED REDEMPTION FORGOTTEN AND REDISCOVERED

We venture now to trace the doctrine of limited redemption through the middle ages, and to build a bridge from Augustine to Calvin.

In his own lifetime Augustine had a "party" of supporters in his conflict with the Pelagians. One of these was Prosper of Aquitaine, a lay monk of Marseilles, who died some time after 455.

It is clear from the early writings of Prosper that the doctrine of limited redemption was perceived as Augustine's own teaching, by adherents and foes alike. Two of the anti-Augustinian sources with which Prosper took issue, the **Capitula Gallorum** and the **Capitula objectionum Vincentianarum**, objected forthrightly against Augustine that his view of salvation limits the extent of the death of Christ to the predestined.[1] And Prosper undertook to defend Augustine with the exegetical devices that Augustine himself had provided: the two-worlds schema,[2] the concept of exclusive universalism,[3] and the the concept of universalism of kinds as a explanation for I Timothy 2:4.[4]

But Prosper is also something of an enigma, for he seems to have moved gradually away from a strict Augustinianism. In the

---

[1] "Objectio: quod non pro totius mundi redemptione Salvator sit crucifixus . . . Objectio: quod Dominus noster Jesus Christus non pro omnium hominum salute et redemptione sit passus." **MPL** 51: 164, 177. Prosper quotes these objections and then responds to them.

[2] **MPL** 51:172.

[3] **MPL** 51:177-8.

[4] **MPL** 51:163.

work entitled **De vocatione omnium gentium** he made assertions
of the death of Christ for all individuals,[1] and gave an
interpretation of I Tim. 2:4 which views God's saving will as being
for all "both in general and in particular."[2] The reasons for this
change are beyond our reach. But Prosper's pilgrimage from a
strict to a more attenuated form of Augustinianism is a parable of
what would happen on a larger scale.

The Augustinian Synthesis

In the place of a discredited Pelagianism arose the hybrid
"Semipelagianism." According to its spokesmen, John Cassian (d.
ca. 435) and Faustus of Riez (d. sometime before 500), grace is
necessary but operates in conjunction with the human will, and
predestination is based on God's foresight of human decision and
merit. Semipelagianism was obviously inimical to the doctrine of
limited redemption. There were still a few strict Augustinians
around, Fulgentius of Ruspe (d. 532), for example, who was a
bishop in Augustine's old province of Africa, since overrun by
Vandals. Fulgentius was a blunt defender of limited redemption,
and appealed, as Augustine had, to the divine omnipotence, and
interpreted important texts like I Timothy 2:4 and John 12:32 as
Augustine had.[3].

But the resolution of the challenge posed by Semipelagianism
would belong, not to men like Fulgentius, but to another
synthesis, a modified Augustinianism which emphasized man's need
for divine grace but muted the bolder implications of Augustine's
theology, viz., reprobation and limited redemption. After a war of
books, the victory of this modified Augustinianism was
consolidated at the Council of Orange in 529.[4] The twenty-five

---

[1] **MPL** 51:702-3.

[2] **MPL** 51:706.

[3] **CCSL** 91A:455, 611. Cf. also **CCSL** 91A:610 for a similar comment
on I Tim. 2:4.

[4] The pronouncements of the Synod of Orange, with an analysis and
historical background, are contained in Carl Joseph Hefele, **Histoire de
Conciles d'après les documents originaux**, 10 vols., trans. Henri Leclercq
(Paris: Letouzey et Ané, Editeurs, 1907-52), 2.2:1085-1110.

canons of Orange asserted the primacy of grace and repudiated the anthropology of Semipelagianism, but left a whole complex of related questions, which had since Augustine been part of the debates, unaddressed and unresolved. Among these was the question of the extent of redemption, about which the canons said absolutely nothing.

Jaroslav Pelikan has seen here the formation of what he calls the "Augustinian synthesis," the blending of Augustine and other ideas which took place as Augustine was dealt with by successive generations of commentators. Perhaps "truncated Augustinianism" is a better term. So completely did the idea of limited redemption fall from view as a result of this truncation that it was possible for a ninth-century theologian, Hincmar of Reims, to regard it in his own day as a "modern" innovation.[1]

But the doctrine was still there, in Augustine's writings, waiting to be rediscovered and reasserted. The monks managed to copy Augustine's works and pass them along to posterity. But it was not until the modest revival of learning that took place under the *pax carolingia* of the early ninth century, in the monasteries and cathedral schools, that someone perceived the forgotten emphases of his theology, including the doctrine of limited redemption. In a strange foreshadowing of the Reformation, the ninth century's disturber of the peace was a Saxon monk.

Gottschalk

Gottschalk of Orbais (d. ca. 869) seemed predestined for conflict with the Roman Catholic authorities of his day. To begin with, he collided with the church over the custom of child oblation--(usually noble) parents dedicating their young children to the monastic life. Gottschalk's father, a Saxon count named Berno, had dedicated the child Gottschalk to the Fulda monastery. As an adult monk, Gottschalk fought his abbot, Raban Maur, to be released from his monastic vows, and in 829 the Synod of Mainz granted Gottschalk's request. But this was only the beginning of troubles.

Gottschalk traveled extensively, to Italy, and even to the

---

[1] J. Pelikan, 3:81.

borders of the Byzantine empire where he attempted to convert
the Bulgars to Christianity. He also studied Augustine's writings,
becoming what we have called a strict Augustinian and therefore
an advocate of limited redemption. This set the stage for his next
collision with the church. Reports of his activity and doctrine
reached Germany and France; Raban Maur then fired the first
salvo of what was to be a long battle when he wrote a piece
against Gottschalk's doctrine of predestination, with the result that
Gottschalk was brought before the Synod of Quiercy (849) on
charges of heresy. Augustine's undiluted predestinarianism was
once again out in the open.

Gottschalk saw himself as the heir of the true and Catholic
theological tradition, which he found in Augustine. He boldly and
incessantly stated his belief that Christ had died only for the elect;
what had been always present but only occasionally explicit in
Augustine, Gottschalk brought to the fore. So it required no
particular perceptiveness for Gottschalk's opponents to note this
doctrine in his theology and use it against him, as had Augustine's
opponents in the fifth century.

In his defense of limited redemption, Gottschalk, predictably,
used the methods of Augustine. He was especially fond of the two-
worlds concept with its definition of the number of the
predestined as the "world" which Christ redeemed with his blood.
Of the two worlds, "Christ is the redeemer, savior, and liberator,
not of both but of one, that is, only of the elect world which is
clearly his own body."[1] To the statement that Christ has suffered
for all (*pro cunctis*), Gottschalk replied that by *cunctis* all the elect
must be understood; there exist two bodies, he explained, one of
Christ and the other of Antichrist, and it is clear that Christ did
not suffer for the body of Antichrist. These two bodies are to be
identified with the two worlds of which scripture speaks;
Gottschalk quoted Augustine to confirm this distinction.[2]

Along these same lines, Gottschalk consistently argued that

---

[1] Cyrille Lambot, ed. **Oeuvres théologiques et grammaticale de Godescalc l'Orbais** (Louvain, 1945), p. 182.

[2] Lambot, pp. 203-4. Gottschalk also made the same appeal to Augustine's two-worlds concept (Lambot, pp. 230-1).

the scriptural passages which speak of universal redemption (e.g. John 12:32, I John 2:2, and I Tim. 2:4) must be understood of all the elect, not of all men without distinction. In truth, Gottschalk did not devote much time to the explanation of such passages. He included John 12:32 and I John 2:2 in a rather matter of fact way in his list of prooftexts for (!) limited redemption, as if it were apparent to any reasonable person that such passages must refer only to the elect.[1] Similarly, regarding I Tim. 2:4, Gottschalk maintained with Augustine that Paul speaks here only of those whom God wills to save, not of everyone,[2] and consequently the verse became, along with others like it, a prooftext for, not against limited redemption.

This plundering of the enemy's best weapons for his own use was not an attempt of Gottschalk's to skirt the issues or to win the debate by calling black white. He believed, by the time he came to such passages, that the debate had already been settled at a more fundamental level. The issue was for him not simply for whom Christ died, but what was nature of Christ's redemptive act. This was apparent in his analysis of redemption itself, where he took the Augustinian tenet of God's omnipotence and applied it to the meaning of Christ's sacrifice.

For the main pillars of Gottschalk's doctrine of limited redemption were not the predestination texts of the Bible--as if limited redemption were a simple deduction from predestination--but redemption texts like Galatians 3:13 ff., Romans 5:8-9, 8:31-32, and II Cor. 5:19.

Concerning the redemption of the elect alone, the apostle Paul says, "Christ redeemed us from the curse of the law, being made a curse for us" (Gal. 3:13).

What does this verse have to do with limited redemption? Gottschalk explained: If the reprobate were redeemed from the curse of the law, they would no longer be cursed, but blessed; yet, Christ will say to them on the last day, "Depart from me, cursed

---

[1] Lambot, pp. 199, 203.
[2] Lambot, p. 237.

ones, into the eternal fire" (Matt. 25:41). Gottschalk reasoned that it is impossible for the reprobate to be, simultaneously, blessed and cursed, delivered from the curse by Christ and cursed by Christ.[1] Likewise, on the basis of Romans 8:31-32 ("If God did not spare his own Son but delivered him up for us all, will he not also with him freely give us all things?"), Gottschalk concluded that since all things (i.e. eternal life) are not in fact given to the reprobate, Christ cannot have been delivered up for them. And if Christ had died for the reprobate, they would be, according to Romans 5:8-9, also saved from the wrath to come. If they were part of the world which Christ reconciled by his death, spoken of in II Cor. 5:19, they would be in fact reconciled.[2]

Gottschalk was conscious of his own logic. In yet another treatment of Gal. 3:13, he identified it as a "syllogism," and set it out as follows: the first truth is that Christ's death redeems from the curse of the law; the second truth is that the reprobate are cursed; the conclusion must be that Christ did not deliver the reprobate from the curse. Foundational to this line of reasoning was Gottschalk's understanding of Christ's redemption as an objective transaction between the Father and the Son. For Gottschalk, what transpired on the cross was not something which merely rendered men *redeemable*, pending the fulfillment of some further condition, but a redemption which *redeemed*. It was, like the will of God, effectual.

If, in regard to the exegesis of the words "all" and "world," Gottschalk's (and Augustine's) opponents could accuse him of not taking the Scripture at face value, here the shoe was on the other foot. Here it was Gottschalk who took the biblical words in their most direct and uncomplicated sense, and the advocates of universal redemption who had to read verses like Gal. 3:13 always with a hidden agenda. For the universal redemptionist, a statement like "Christ redeemed us . . . " has always to be accompanied by a silent *if*, since not all whom Christ redeemed finally are redeemed. With this kind of contingency Gottschalk, as an Augustinian, would have nothing to do. He could not think in

[1] Lambot, p. 157.
[2] Lambot, p. 158.

terms of possible or potential salvation. And consequently, since it is clear that not all men are finally redeemed, it followed for him that Christ did not redeem them. He even preferred, with Origen, the doctrine of universal salvation, since at least on this scheme of things the blood of Christ is not wasted and the saving will of God is not ineffectual.[1] One must in any case be able to say that what God intends to do through the death of Christ *is* done. That was the very heart of Gottschalk's doctrine of the death of Christ. All else flowed from it.

Gottschalk's linking of the extent of redemption to the nature of redemption anticipated the thought of Bucer and Calvin, who would use the language of *satisfactio* which Anselm provided in the meantime, and also of Beza, who would argue for limited redemption from the denial of "double payment."

If Gottschalk was in so many respects a faithful follower of Augustine, there was one notable omission, namely, the absence of Augustine's effort to somehow preserve the universalistic thrust of verses like John 12:32 and I Tim. 2:4. One finds no trace in Gottschalk of Augustine's universalism of kinds; "all" and "world" were simply reduced, without further ado, to the elect. So he failed to provide any explanation for why such verses do not simply *say* "the elect" instead of "all." This was a significant omission from the Augustinian doctrine of limited redemption, and one which would not be made by most of those who followed in the same tradition, including Calvin.

Gottschalk was not alone in his defense of limited redemption. Indeed, not until the Reformation would the defense of limited redemption again take on the character of a "movement" as it did in the ninth century. Among Gottschalk's supporters were Ratramnus (d. ca. 868), an early teacher of Gottschalk's who probably influenced him in his theological development, Remigius of Lyon (d. 875)[2] and his brilliant deacon Florus (d. ca. 860),

---

[1] Lambot, p. 249.

[2] It was a strange twist of history when the remains of Remigius, who was in his day a defender of the theology of grace which would later be called "Calvinism," were destroyed by the Huguenots in 1562. **Lexikon für Theologie und Kirche**, 11 vols. (Freiburg: Verlag Herder, 1957-67) 8:1226.

many of whose writings were until recently attributed to Remigius,[1] Prudentius of Troyes (d. 861), and Lupus of Ferrières (d. sometime after 862). These friends of Gottschalk argued for limited redemption with the familiar Augustinian methods.[2] Among Gottschalk and his supporters there was also an appeal to the biblical term "many," as it is used several times in the New Testament in connection with redemption, most notably in the words of the institution of the Lord's Supper (Matt. 26, Mark 14), when Jesus says that the cup is his blood which is poured out for many. Prudentius and Florus both see this as a reference to the elect.[3] This interpretation of "many" would become a fairly common exegetical procedure among limited redemptionists, but one, for reasons which will be explained, that Calvin would refuse to utilize.

Gottschalk was the leader of a vigorous movement. But this movement also had powerful and articulate enemies, notably Raban Maur, abbot of Fulda and later bishop of Mainz (d. 856), and Hincmar, bishop of Reims (d. 882). Hincmar and Raban Maur countered Gottschalk from several angles. As might be expected, they adduced the universalistic redemption statements of the Bible to refute the concept of limited redemption. Raban Maur brought I Tim. 2:6, the "ransom for all" passage, into the debate.[4] This was old ground. There were two other objections to limited redemption which we must mention because of their anticipation of issues which would exercise Calvin. First, Hincmar pointed out the statement of Paul about the brother perishing for whom Christ died (I Cor. 8:11),[5] and argued, with good logic, that if someone for whom Christ died can perish, then the extent of redemption cannot be limited just to the elect. He was saying, to put this another way, that I Cor. 8:11 cancels out the basic premise of Gottschalk, that redemption in the Bible is always efficacious. To Hincmar, the verse proved that the death of Christ provides

---

[1] Lexikon 8:1225-6.
[2] MPL 119:645; 121:1011-12; 121:1124; 121:1125.
[3] MPL 115:976-77, 121:1125.
[4] MPL 112:1527.
[5] MPL 125:309.

potential but not inevitable redemption. Gottschalk replied to this objection by saying that the larger body of prooftexts about the efficacy of redemption must be allowed to interpret this one, and gave a somewhat strained exegesis of the passage.[1] But this was to beg the question, not to answer it. Calvin, facing the same biblical teaching--which occurs in more instances than just I Cor. 8:11-- would deal with it in a much different, and more practical, manner.

Second, Gottschalk's opponents objected that the doctrine of limited redemption militates against the objective grace of baptism. Amolus of Lyons asked: if Christ's blood is always effectual for redemption (as Gottschalk maintained), and if some who are baptized perish, then must we not conclude that the price of Christ's blood was not really given at baptism?[2] This was a serious and fundamental objection, one that put Gottschalk in a quandary and forced him to desperate devices, one of which was a semantic solution: "redemption" has several meanings; there is indeed a redemption which is given through baptism, but it is not that full redemption which saves men eternally.[3] So Gottschalk's doctrine of baptism came to look very much like Hincmar's doctrine of the death of Christ itself--it communicates a redemption which does not always redeem. Gottschalk's solution cannot conceal the fact that there was a real tension between a consistent predestinarian soteriology and a soteriology in which grace is objectively mediated through the church and its sacraments. And both of these conceptions were traceable to Augustine himself. Gottschalk was caught between them. He was an Augustinian, but he was no Protestant. We shall elaborate later on the thesis that Reformed theology was the first truly decisive resolution of this tension.

The ninth century predestinarian struggle was a bitter affair which generated a long series of councils--Quiercy (849), second Quiercy (853), Toul (859), and Toucy (860) which pronounced

---

[1] Lambot, p. 216.

[2] Amolus of Lyon, in **Monumenta Germaniae Historica, Epistolae** 5:371, and Hincmar, **MPL** 125:365.

[3] Lambot, pp. 221-2.

against Gottschalk and limited redemption,[1] and Paris (849), Sens (853), and Valence (855) which pronounced for limited redemption. From 849, Gottschalk carried on his struggle from prison; along the way most of his influential supporters died; in 869 he died, having been denied Christian burial by Hincmar.

The muzzling of Gottschalk encapsulated what had happened: once again Augustine's theology of grace had been taken out of mothballs, passionately argued, and squelched. And the doctrine of limited redemption would continue to be in the wings, rather than on center stage, of Catholic theology.

[1] Cf. Hefele, 2.2:198 for a statement of the theology inspired by Hincmar and stated by the synods which he controlled.

4

SCHOLASTICISM: LIMITED REDEMPTION SURVIVES ANOTHER SYNTHESIS

The history of strict Augustinianism in the period of "scholastic" theology (ca.1000-1500) bears a striking resemblance to its history in the preceding period. Historical "parallels" are always inexact, and drawing lessons from them extremely risky. What happened, however, is fairly clear. In the high middle ages there was another great and influential "Augustinian synthesis" (as there had been at Orange in the sixth century) in which the doctrine of limited redemption was submerged; in the later middle ages there was a revival of strict Augustinianism, including limited redemption, which was perceived, as the Gottschalk movement had been, as a serious threat to the institutional church.

Limited redemption continued to find advocates in the so-called "age of scholasticism." Clear articulations of limited redemption are to be found in Haymo, an abbot of the eleventh century,[1] whose language closely reflected Augustine's, and in Guibert of Nogent (d. 1124).[2] Augustine's exegesis of I Tim. 2:4 also continued to find expression in the early scholastics. Anselm, for instance, limited the saving will of God to the "righteous,"[3] and Hugh of St. Victor, building on the conviction that what God wills must take place, followed Augustine in seeing the saving will of God in I Tim. 2:4 as the power by which God makes men

---

[1] **MPL** 117:789-90. The works which, in **MPL** 117, are attributed to Haymo of Halberstadt, a ninth-century bishop, are probably those of an eleventh-century monk of the same name. Cf. Hauck, **Kirchengeschichte Deutschlands**, 5 vols. (Berlin: Akademie Verlag, 1903-20), 2:579.

[2] **MPL** 156:635.

[3] **MPL** 158:488.

willing to be saved.[1] This is, in effect, to limit it to the elect, since
God does not work this desire in any but the elect. Peter Lombard
especially showed himself repeatedly a faithful disciple of
Augustine in this regard. He often asserted Augustine's doctrine
of the divine omnipotence,[2] and made it the foundation both of
his exposition of I Tim. 2:4 and of his systematic treatment of the
question of God's will in the **Sentences**:

> "Who wills all men to be saved." Because of these words many
> have deviated from the truth, saying that God wills many things
> to happen which do not happen. But it must not for this reason
> be understood to speak as if God willed some to be saved and
> they are not saved.[3]

Accordingly, the Lombard explained the passage using both
Augustine's exclusive universalism[4] and his universalism of kinds.[5]

But strict Augustinianism was not to be the theology of the
day. That honor belonged to the carefully balanced system of
Thomas Aquinas.

Thomas Aquinas

Thomas was unquestionably an Augustinian in the broad
sense. He strove always to establish the primacy and necessity of
grace, and his doctrine of predestination was wholly Augustinian.
He rejected, for example, the notion that predestination is based
on God's foreknowlege of human action, a notion which had been
a favorite with Gottschalk's foes. However, in his doctrine of the
death of Christ he did in fact take a different direction from
Augustine, one that appears to have been determined by his desire
to say, in some sense, that God's saving will and act are intended
for every individual. At the same time, as a predestinarian, he had
to maintain the particularity of salvation for the elect. The effort

---

[1] MPL 176:65.
[2] MPL 192:636.
[3] MPL 192:645.
[4] MPL 192:6435.
[5] MPL 192:338.

to synthesize these concerns led Thomas to a synthesis which he achieved with the help of two logical distinctions.

The first of these related to the exegesis of I Tim. 2:4, always a lodestone. The simple solution of Augustine--that God does *not* will the salvation of all men--did not completely satisfy Thomas. He preferred the very different kind of explanation which came, not from Augustine, but from Chrysostom, namely, the distinction between the antecedent and consequent wills of God, the purpose of which was to enable the interpreter to say both that God wills the salvation of all men and that all men are not saved--all of this, ostensibly, without reflecting badly on the omnipotence of God. The distinction had been adopted by John of Damascus, the great eighth-century systematizer of Eastern theology, through whom it was transmitted west in the 13th century when many of the Damascene's works were translated into Latin. Albertus Magnus adopted it as his explanation of I Tim. 2:4, to the exclusion of the Augustinian exegesis.[1] Thomas himself gave the doctor of Hippo his due by including Augustine's universalism of kinds explanation in his reply to the standard question, whether the will of God is always fulfilled,[2] but also put alongside it the explanation based on the antecedent-consequent distinction. Which of these explanations did he prefer? The answer comes later in the **Summa** when Thomas poses I Tim. 2:4 as a potential objection to the doctrine of predestination, and answers:

> God wills all men to be saved by his antecedent will, which is to will not simply but relatively; and not by his consequent will, which is to will simply.[3]

God wills all men to be saved, that is, *if* they accept the grace of

---

[1] **Sent.** 1.40.8.

[2] Thomas Aquinas, **Summa Theologica** (after this cited as **S.T.**) 1.19.6. Thomas here provided a formulation of the Augustinian universalism of kinds exegesis which would be used later by limited redemptionists, including Calvin: the saving will of God is distributed *pro generibus singulorum, et non pro singulis generum.*

[3] **S.T.** 1.23.4.

Christ. According to Thomas, it is this universal, conditional saving will of God that I Tim. 2:4 describes, and therefore for him the verse posed no objection to predestination, since predestination is God's simple will. So Thomas salvaged predestination. But in the process he sacrificed the Augustinian axiom that God's will to save must always be effectual. Augustine, it will be remembered, had made this the one necessary rule to be observed in the interpretation of the passage. That Thomas broke it is testimony to the independence of his theological thinking.

What place then did the death of Christ occupy in Thomas' theology? Did it carry out the antecedent will of God as an act of salvation for all, or did it carry out the simple, predestinating will of God for the elect? Here again Thomas displayed his genius for synthesis by preserving a part of each. This necessitated the use of a second logical distinction: that Christ died "sufficiently" for all men but "efficiently" only for the elect.

The terminology was not original with Thomas.[1] But Thomas harnessed it to universalize the saving will of God in the death of Christ. That Christ died sufficiently meant for him that God really wills to save all men through the death of Christ. "Christ's passion is sufficient for all for the forgiveness of sins and the attaining of grace and glory."[2] Thomas located the objective work of satisfaction here in the sufficient sacrifice of Christ for all: "By his passion Christ has made satisfaction for the sin of the human race."[3] It should be added here too that when Thomas said "all" and "human race" he meant all individuals. In contrast to Gottschalk, who had insisted that the payment of debt at the cross was made only for the elect, Thomas declared:

> Christ's passion was a sufficient and superabundant satisfaction for the sins of the whole human race; but when sufficient satisfaction has been paid, then the debt of punishment is abolished.[4]

[1] Peter Damian, in **MPL** 145:884.
[2] S.T. 3.79.7.
[3] S.T. 3.46.1.
[4] S.T. 3.49.3.

So the whole race, including both the elect and the reprobate, has had its legal-penal obligation satisfied by the death of Christ. We are here within a very different theological structure from that of Augustine and Gottschalk. Uncertainty about Thomas' position is virtually eliminated when we observe how Thomas consistently treated the biblical statements which had so concerned Augustine and other limited redemptionists, statements like John 12:32 and I John 2:2. Thomas simply took them as statements of Christ's death for all individuals.[1] He felt no need to comment further on them, or to use any of the exegeses that had become standard with limited redemptionists, because they posed no challenge to his theology, as they did for limited redemptionists. It is true that in his exegesis of I Tim. 2:4, already noted, Thomas included the Augustinian interpretation among possible interpretations, though in the end he did not prefer it. The fact that he did not utilize it in his treatment of other similar texts simply underscores his distance from Augustine on this point.

Later limited redemptionists would find their own way to utilize the sufficient-efficient distinction. But the interpretation of the "all" and "world" passages would continue to set them apart from universal redemptionists.

Christ has satisfied for the sins of all. But for Thomas this did not mean that all men are saved. Something else must take place, and it is here that the concept of the efficiency of Christ's death comes into play. Not only must satisfaction be made, but man must be personally united to Christ.

> Christ's passion works its effect in them to whom it is applied, through faith and charity, and the sacraments of faith . . . In order to secure the effects of Christ's passion we must be made like unto him . . . Christ's satisfaction works its effect in us inasmuch as we are incorporated with him.[2]

All men are not saved. But the elect are saved as the death of Christ is applied to them.

[1] S.T. 3.48.2.
[2] S.T. 3.49.3.

The blood of Christ's passion has its efficacy not merely in the elect among the Jews, to whom the blood of the Old Testament was exhibited, but also in the Gentiles.[1]

Christ's passion sufficed for all, while as to its efficacy it was profitable to many.[2]

The limited redemptionist also believed, of course, that the benefits of Christ's passion must be personally applied and communicated. But for the limited redemptionist there was a necessary connection and coextensiveness between the death of Christ and its application; for Thomas there was not. For the limited redemptionist, the death of Christ and its application had one scope, the elect; for Thomas, there existed a category of people for whom Christ died but to whom the benefits of his death never come.

Thomas was, in short, a genuine predestinarian who was also a universal redemptionist, and as such he was the precursor of Moyse Amyraut.

John Wyclif

Thomas' great synthesis was being questioned almost before the ink was dry on the **Summa Theologica**, and scholastic theology after 1300 became a complex mosaic. Among the dissatisfied were a small number of strict Augustinians, latter-day Gottschalks, willing to follow Augustine "all the way" (Pelikan's phrase). Among these theologians there was a return to Augustine's exegesis of I Tim. 2:4 and to his doctrine of limited redemption. The doctrine survived the Thomistic synthesis just as it had the synods of Orange and Toucy.

The gospel of these "latter-day Augustinians" was often articulated in *Auseinandersetzung* with what they perceived to be the revival of Pelagianism in their own day. And it is true that in

---

[1] S.T. 3.78.3.
[2] S.T. 3.78.3. Cf. also **Super Epistola S. Pauli lectura** (Romae: Marietti, 1953), p. 440.

the theological approach which has come to be known as "nominalism" there was a strong emphasis on the capability of the human will. Thomas Bradwardine, one of these Augustinians, entitled his most important theological work **The Cause of God Against the Pelagians.**[1] This cause, according to Bradwardine, was the cause of double predestination and the utter impotence of the human will to move itself toward God without divine grace. But the prevailing view stressed God's universal love and saving will, and tended to ascribe the reason for the difference between the saved and the lost, not to God, but to man.

Here I Tim. 2:4 once more became a storm center. The spokesmen for the prevailing viewpoint understood the verse to be speaking of all men individually and without differentiation, of "Judas as well as Peter,[2]" to put it most bluntly. And the antecedent-consequent distinction was commonly used to salvage the efficacy of the divine will from such an exegesis.[3] Gregory of Rimini, however, saw in such a treatment of the verse the ghost of Pelagius and the seeds of the exaltation of the human will at the expense of the divine, and so returned to Augustine's interpretation. Rejecting the antecedent-consequent scheme along with its motive, he maintained that "all" means all categories of men and that the saving will of God is for the elect from these categories:

> The sense is that God wills some to be saved from every estate, whether noble or ignoble, poor or rich, male or female, and of

---

[1] Cf. Gordon Leff, **Bradwardine and the Pelagians: A Study of his 'De Causa Dei' and its Opponents** (Cambridge, 1957).

[2] Cf. for example Peter Aureolus: I **Sent.** d. XLI, 940bB. Quoted in Paul Vignaux, **Justification et prédestination au XIVe Siecle** (Paris: Libraire Ernest Leroux, 1934), p. 49.

[3] Giles of Rome, Duns Scotus, and William of Ockham, for example, all utilized the antecedent-consequent distinction. Cf. G. Leff, **Gregory of Rimini: Tradition and Innovation in Fourteenth Century Thought** (Manchester, 1961), p. 199.

whatever differences there are among individuals.[1]

Gregory also used a formula which Aquinas had provided and which Calvin would use as well, which states that the universality of the saving will of God *sit distributio pro generibus singulorum non pro singulis omnium generum* (is distributed to kinds of individuals not to all individuals of a kind).[2] Thomas, as a collector of numerous (and sometimes mutually contradictory) proofs, had cited this interpretation, obviously Augustine's, but had not adopted it. But for Gregory of Rimini it was the one correct explanation.

Nor did the late medieval Augustinians halt on the brink of the master's teaching on limited redemption.

Bradwardine was carried off in the Black Death of 1349, but an English defense of strict soteriological Augustinianism was continued in the person of John Wyclif, who managed--one would suspect only because it was predestined--to die a natural death despite his ferocious attack on the doctrine and structure of the Catholic church of the late fourteenth century. Wyclif was a limited redemptionist, but his expression of the doctrine showed that five centuries of theologizing had gone by since Gottschalk. The Saxon monk had stated his doctrine without frills; the Oxford doctor worked within a well-established scholastic tradition. He delighted in chopping logic and in multiplying distinctions, and his train of thought was often heavy going. His position on limited redemption contained an angle unknown to Augustine or Gottschalk.

Wyclif affirmed the omnipotence of God and the doctrine of predestination in the strongest conceivable terms. The divine will is immutable.[3] He was not reticent to say that because of God's predestination all things happen by necessity, since it is impossible

---

[1] Sent. dist. 46 et 47, q. 1, **Gregorii Ariminensis Oesa Lectura super Primum et Secundum Sententiarum** (Berlin and New York: De Gruyter, 1984), p. 517.

[2] **Gregorii Ariminensis**, p. 517.

[3] **Wyclif's Latin Works**, 35 vols. (London, 1883-1914) 10:79. After this cited as **WLW**.

for the divine will to be frustrated or altered;[1] even the fall of Adam into sin was in this sense necessary.[2]

Given these premises, it is not surprising that Wyclif's conception of history was also framed by the doctrine of predestination and by the Augustinian conception of two parallel, intermingled, but inimical human societies, the elect and the reprobate, moving inexorably to their appointed goals. His favorite terms for these two groups were *predestinati* and *presciti*, the predestined and the foreknown.[3] The predestined were for Wyclif the true church, and on this definition of the church as the "congregation of all the predestined"[4] he built his challenge to the secular-institutional form which the church of his day had assumed. His famous treatise **De ecclesia** began with this definition and flowed logically from it.

Wyclif's predestinarian ecclesiology was also closely tied to Christology. For the two humanities have as their respective heads the devil and Christ. Therefore the "body of the devil" (the *presciti*) and the "body of Christ (the *predestinati*) are as incapable of assimilation or mixture as the heads to which they belong. Wyclif's theology thus posited an exclusive relationship between Christ and the predestined: they alone are the bride which he has loved from eternity, has espoused to himself, and will perfect on the last day. It is, said Wyclif, impossible for Christ ever not to love the predestinate, just as it is impossible for him ever to love the reprobate.[5] He appealed frequently to the Song of Songs (allegorically interpreted) and to Paul's declaration that Christ "loved the church and gave himself up for her" (Ephesians 5:25).[6]

---

[1] **WLW** 21.1:231.

[2] **WLW** 21.1:236.

[3] Technically, for Wyclif the *presciti* were a subcategory of the *reprobati*, specifically, those who are included in the visible church but who are not predestined. He spoke more often of the *presciti* because this category was a more immediate reality in a society which considered itself "Catholic." For purposes of this study, the two terms are interchangeable.

[4] **WLW** 10:2.

[5] **WLW** 10:79.

[6] Cf. **WLW** 10:80.

As might be expected, such a conception of the union of Christ with the church led for Wyclif to the doctrine of limited redemption. "It should be believed in faith that Christ made satisfaction for all his members."[1] Having quoted Eph. 5:25, Wyclif commented:

> [Here] there is no doubt but that he speaks, by way of limitation (*limitate*), of the church which is the corporation of the predestined, for this is the church he redeemed, it he will glorify after the day of judgment, it will then have no spot or wrinkle, and it is the body of Christ which he cherishes and loves.[2]

As a limited redemptionist, Wyclif had the usual task of explaining the universalistic passages of the New Testament. The doctrine of John 3:16, that God loves the "world," must be handled carefully, said Wyclif, since "world" has different meanings. There is a world which God loves and saves, which consists of the predestinate, and another which he damns.[3] So he suggested that the "world" of John 3:16 is the as yet unconverted elect who still wander, as it were, in the wilderness of the world.[4] It is quite clear that it could not mean for Wyclif every human being. And underlying this two-worlds idea, as might be expected, was the Augustinian doctrine of the omnipotence of the divine will, which Wyclif appended to this same comment: "God's purpose cannot be frustrated."[5] This principle dictates that all whom God loves and wants to save, be saved. Likewise, according to Wyclif, the predestinate were entrusted by the Father to the Son for the purpose of redemption, and it is therefore impossible that any of those thus given to the Son should perish in the day of judgment.[6] It follows that the *praesciti* are not objects of redemption: "No one whom he foreknows to damnation does he

---

[1] **WLW** 10:557.
[2] **WLW** 10:439-40.
[3] **WLW** 21.4:83.
[4] **WLW** 21.4:82.
[5] **WLW** 21.4:84.
[6] **WLW** 21.4:90.

redeem."[1]

If Wyclif was in these fundamental respects a faithful disciple of Augustine, in certain ways his theological thinking shows to what extent he was a scholastic theologian. When he interpreted I Timothy 2:4, for example, he did not use Augustine's simple approach based on the omnipotence of God and a universalism of kinds; instead, in good scholastic fashion, he defined four senses of "salvation," only the third and fourth of which are eternal salvation, and stated that the will of God in I Tim. 2:4 is connected only with these.[2] The end result was, of course, that which Augustine would have desired, but the method was scholastic.

Wyclif also used the sufficient-efficient schema to analyse the death of Christ, for which he was, of course, indebted to Thomas Aquinas. Wyclif granted, as had Thomas, that the death of Christ was sufficient for the entire human race; this was part of his exegesis of I John 2:2:

> For Christ is, as far as sufficiency, a propitiation, that is, a propitiating doctor or medicine for the whole human race.[3]

Wyclif sounded like Thomas here, but his meaning was different; he was appropriating Thomas' terms for his own use. For Wyclif the concept of sufficiency meant, not that Christ satisfied and obtained redemption for all men (as it had for Thomas), but rather that the passion of Christ, considered *in ipso*, had virtue enough for the whole world, or many worlds, as many as God might will to save through it.[4] So it was the same word that Thomas used, but a different concept.

This concept of the theoretical sufficiency of Christ's sacrifice led Wyclif to posit something which Augustine had not imagined: non-saving benefits of redemption for the non-elect. For the elect Christ has obtained eternal life, beatitude. For the reprobate,

[1] **WLW** 21.4:90.
[2] **WLW** 10:60.
[3] **WLW** 10:60.
[4] **WLW** 10:59.

however, Christ has acquired, not eternal life, but the mitigation of punishment, both temporal and eternal. Wyclif called this a "secondary perfection" flowing from the passion of Christ.[1] Because even the reprobate are the brothers of Christ in the sense that he shares their nature, Wyclif was willing to grant *equivocando* (by way of double meaning) that "he punishes his own brothers more mercifully for their own good, as I have said in other places."[2] By virtue of Christ's death it is possible to speak of a "present righteousness" in the foreknown, which however, does not persevere. Therefore the foreknown person merits, not eternal beatitude, but

> the perpetual mitigation of eternal punishment along with other temporal goods; and thus God redeems the foreknown not to beatitude but to the mitigation of eternal punishment, just as he redeems all the damned.[3]

It is with reference to the secondary but nonredemptive benefits of Christ's death to the damned that Wyclif handled the verse John 12:32, "I will draw all men to myself."[4]

So, in the end, what Wyclif granted to the damned from the death of Christ was simply the softening of their punishment in hell, along with certain temporal--and temporary--blessings. So, in spite of a few scholastic accretions, Wyclif carried on Augustine's limitation of the death of Christ to the predestined.

John Hus

The same was true of Wyclif's most famous disciple, John Hus.

In Hus's longest theological work, his comments on the **Sentences** of Peter Lombard (**Super IV. Sententiarum**, compiled in the course of university instruction from 1407-9), it is not easy

---

[1] **WLW** 10:57.

[2] **WLW** 10:59.

[3] **WLW** 10:468. Other statements of this doctrine may be found in **WLW** 10:358, 497, 531, 21.2:174, 21.4:90.

[4] **WLW** 21.2:173-4.

to tell exactly where he stood on the extent of redemption. His treatment of I Timothy 2:4 introduced several approaches and made no commitment.[1] His answer to the question, whether the blood of Christ blots out all sins, was also noncommital,[2] as was his approach to the straight-out question: did Christ die only for the elect?[3] It is difficult to know whether Hus's ambiguity in this work was the product of real ambiguity in his own thinking or simply a pedagogical tool to stimulate the thinking of his students. Whatever the case with his commentary on the **Sentences**, there is no doubt where he stood in his most famous work, **De ecclesia**, written in 1412-13.

In **De ecclesia**, Hus followed Wyclif, often using the Englishman's very words. He defined the church as the body of the predestinate, over which Christ is the head and for which he shed his blood,

> the number of all the predestinate and the mystical body of Christ, whose head he is and the bride whom, of his great love, he redeemed with his blood.[4]

Hus adopted Wyclif's doctrine that the death of Christ achieves for the reprobate only the mitigation of punishment. Following closely Wyclif's treatment of Thomas, Hus says, using Wyclif's very words, that *cum virtute passionis Christi acquiritur quedam perfectio secundaria toti mundo*.[5] Then Hus expounded further (Wyclif's words are in italics):

> From these things it appears in what way Christ is the head of all men, and in what way of the predestinate, and in what way *it is not contradictory, by way of double meaning, to call the body of the devil*, that is, the synagogue of Satan, *the church of Christ* because

---

[1] Johann Hus, **Super IV. Sententiarum**, ed. Wenzel Flajshans and Dr. Marie Kominkova (Osnabrück: Biblio-Verlag, 1966), pp. 177-9.

[2] Hus, **Super**, p. 446.

[3] Hus, **Super**, p. 448.

[4] **Magistri Johannis Hus Tractatus de Ecclesia**, ed. S. Harrison Thomson (Boulder, Colo.: University of Colorad Press, 1956), p. 7.

[5] **De Ecclesia**, p. 41.

of the benefits of creation and preservation, not because of the
union of love, in which way the church of Christ is spoken of,
which he loved . . . [1]

The meaning of the death of Christ was logically linked to the
meaning of Christ's headship; since Christ's headship over the
reprobate is not redemptive, the intent of his death for them is
also not redemptive, but has only to do with creation and
preservation. In **De Ecclesia**, at least, Hus was a limited
redemptionist.

The "scholastic" period in perspective

In some ways we should view the late medieval
predestinarians--Gregory of Rimini, Wyclif, Hus--as latter day
Gottschalks. Like Gottschalk, they asserted the particularity of
salvation, and the limitation of Christ's sacrifice to the elect,
against the background of a mediating theological synthesis which
had universalized it.

But the parallel only goes so far. It was a different world, and
a different church, to which Wyclif and Hus spoke. Gottschalk was
simply trying to recover the gospel according to Augustine; Wyclif
and Hus were trying to dismantle the papal monarchy, and their
Augustinian soteriology was a political and ecclesiological weapon.
To define the church as the corporation of the predestined, and
redemption as the gift of Christ only to the predestined, was to
severely undermine the papal church as it had come to define
itself. Wyclif and Hus were taking the machinery of salvation out
of the hands of the hierarchy and giving it back to God.

In addition to this, we can see that the discussion and
formulation of limited redemption, even for its advocates, had
become increasingly complex by the eve of the Reformation.
Distinctions and categories unknown to Augustine or even to
Gottschalk--the antecedent and consequent wills of God, sufficient
and efficient suffering of Christ, non-redemptive benefits of the
death of Christ--formed the stuff of analysis.   We will see Bucer
and Calvin sweep the discussion clean of these devices and return

---

[1] **De ecclesia**, p. 42.

to the exegetical methods of Augustine. This was not necessarily a return to simplicity: Augustine's exegesis was sometimes based on some pretty fine verbal and theological nuances. It was, rather, a return to a soteriology which was uncompromisingly particularistic. It was not part of Augustine's concern to find some "secondary" way to extend the death of Christ to the reprobate, which Wyclif, though a limited redemptionist, tried to do. In this respect, Calvin's doctrine of the extent of redemption would be a return to that of Gottschalk and Augustine.

This is to anticipate something which remains to be proved. Still, the history of the doctrine which has been traced should affect the kinds of assumptions and expectations with which a study of Calvin is approached. For the high predestinarian tradition, in which the doctrine of limited redemption persistently cropped up, was the tradition in which John Calvin stood. Like the other magisterial reformers, Calvin saw himself as a defender of pure Augustinianism against the creeping Pelagianism of the Roman church. Against this background, and in light of the history of predestinarianism before him, it would be a startling surprise to find in Calvin an advocate of universal redemption. Whether this is the case must be determined by a careful investigation of his treatment of the biblical texts, especially of those which had always been the problem of the limited redemptionist position, the universal redemption texts of the New Testament. Having seen how these texts were handled by limited redemptionists for a thousand years, we have a plumbline against which to measure and assess Calvin.

Finally, before leaving the middle ages, we must note again that Thomas Aquinas anticipated the thinking of Moyse Amyraut when he combined double predestination and universal redemption in one theological system. Recent proponents of the Amyraut thesis have treated limited redemption as a "scholastic" dogma; R. T. Kendall seemed to think that Thomas was a limited redemptionist because he used the "sufficient-efficient" schema.[1] The fact is that the word "scholastic" has been loosely thrown around by the scholars more as a perjorative term than as an accurate historical definition. In my opinion, Amyraut has a better claim to it than Beza. But that judgment must await our examination of Calvin's theology.

---

[1] Kendall, p. 18, footnote 2. Kendall was apparently not aware that universal redemptionists used the distinction one way, limited redemptionists another, as we have seen with Wyclif.

5

MARTIN BUCER AND THE DEFENSE OF LIMITED REDEMPTION AGAINST THE ANABAPTISTS

In Martin Bucer we come for the first time to a figure whose theological influence on John Calvin was direct and personal. Calvin knew Augustine well, but only through his books. His knowledge of medieval theology was adequate, though it is doubtful that he knew of Gottschalk, and we do not know if he read Wyclif or Hus. But Bucer he knew as a scholar, a fellow reformer, a friend, and something of a mentor.

Bucer's earliest theological writings as a reformer show him to have been a limited redemptionist.[1] In his 1524 manifesto of the reformed doctrine of the Lord's Supper, **Grund und Ursach**, Bucer returned often to this idea. Christ by his death has made satisfaction for "all the elect."[2] The "many" of Hebrews 9:28 for whom Christ offered himself are, Bucer said, "all the elect,"[3] as are the "sanctified ones" of Hebrews 10:14.[4] The Supper is not a re-sacrificing of Christ but rather a sign of and a participation in the

---

[1] Scholars of Bucer have long been aware of his limitation of the death of Christ to the elect: August Lang, **Der Evangelienkommentar Bucers und die Grundzüge seiner Theologie** (Leipzig, 1900), pp. 164-66; E. Doumergue, **Jean Calvin: Les hommes et les choses de son temps**, 8 vols. (Genève: Slatkin Reprints, 1969), 4:406; François Wendel, **Martin Bucer** (Strasbourg, 1951), p. 20; W. P. Stephens, **The Holy Spirit in the Theology of Martin Bucer** (Cambridge : The University Press, 1970), p. 24.

[2] **Martin Bucers Deutsche Schriften**, 8 vols., ed. Robert Stupperich (Gütersloh: Gerd Mohn, 1960-), 1:212. After this cited as **MBDS**.

[3] **MBDS** 1:213.

[4] **MBDS** 1:213.

one offering "which he himself once offered to his Father on the cross for the sins of all the elect."[1] Although, as we will see, Bucer's fullest defense of limited redemption was occasioned by his conflict with the Anabaptists, the doctrine was not a product of this conflict. As far as we can tell, Bucer began his career as a reformer with the doctrine already in place. It consistently determined the nature of his language when speaking about the purpose of Christ's death.[2]

The Strassburg Anabaptists brought Bucer's doctrine of limited redemption out of the commentaries and into the open light of public debate. Unlike Luther, whose exposure to Anabaptism was entirely second-hand, and Calvin, whose exposure was intense but brief, Bucer's work in Strassburg was pursued for almost twenty years in steady contact and conflict with the bewildering array of radical types that came to Strassburg in the 1520s and 1530s, and especially after 1529, when the Diet of Speyer mandated the death penalty for rebaptism within the empire. That Strassburg was a haven for radicals because of its relatively tolerant policy is well known; that this tolerance was the result of Bucer's own tolerent and irenic spirit is a myth. Henry Krahn has shown conclusively that Bucer pursued a hard line against the radicals, and that it was actually the Town Council which, by refusing to follow the urgings of Bucer and the other preachers, made Strassburg one of the safer cities of the empire for radicals.[3] In Bucer's view, leniency toward the radicals was a great obstacle in the way of true, magisterial-style reformation; he once called it a policy of "longstanding and impious clemency."[4] The Synod of Strassburg of 1533 was something of a victory for the preachers, but even after this, the harshness of treatment of radical types in Strassburg

---

[1] MBDS 1:215.

[2] M. Bucer, **In sacra quatuor evangelia Enarrationes perpetuae** (Basileae: Ioannes Hervagius, 1536), pp. 225, 177, 12.

[3] Henry Krahn, *An Analysis of the Conflict between the Clergy of the Reformed Church and the Leaders of the Anabaptist Movement in Strasbourg, 1524-34* (Ph.D. dissertation, University of Washington, 1969).

[4] Quoted in G. H. Williams, **The Radical Reformation** (Philadelphia: The Westminster Press, 1962), p. 278.

remained less than the norm. Nothing as horrendous as the torture of Michael Sattler in Rottenberg, the drowning of Felix Manz in Zurich, or the burning of Michael Servetus in Geneva, ever transpired in Strassburg during this period.[1]

The Debate with the Anabaptists

Part of the explanation for Bucer's desire to rid Strassburg of Anabaptists was their insistence that Christ died for every human being. The term "Anabaptist," as used here, encompasses a variety of characters and ideas, from Hans Denck the quiet spiritualist to Melchior Hoffmann the eschatological militant. But, whatever other differences separated them from each other, the radicals shared a common front against the Augustinian predestinarian complex of doctrines, and among them limited redemption.

When Hans Denck came to Strassburg from Augsburg in late 1526, he had already published his opposition to the doctrine of limited redemption. In the strong antipredestinarian piece entitled **Was geredt sei**, probably a response to a predestinarian book by Andreas Karlstadt, Denck argued that since God is perfect love, and the nature of love is to exclude none, Christ must have died for all, none excluded.[2] Christ is the mediator between God and men. "Which men? Mine and yours only? No, rather of all men."[3] Bucer's associate, Wolfgang Capito, at first received Denck in friendly fashion, and there is record of a three-way conversation, in Capito's home, among Denck, Capito, and Martin Cellarius. But Bucer perceived Denck immediately as a threat, and arranged a public disputation with him, which took place on December 22-23, 1526. In this debate, the extent of Christ's redemption was one of the points of contention. At the end of the debate, Denck was

---

[1] That is, not for Anabaptism as such. An idiosyncratic visionary named Nicholas Frey was judicially drowned in Strassburg in 1533 for bigamy. Cf. Williams, p. 292. Bucer would later seek to justify the bigamy of Philip of Hesse on biblical grounds!

[2] Hans Denck, **Schriften**, ed. Walter Fellmann (Gütersloh: C. Bertelsmannn Verlag, 1956), p. 39.

[3] Denck, p. 33.

forced out of the city.[1] From there he went to nearby Worms, where he won over to his own view the Lutheran preacher, Jakob Kautz.

In June of 1527, this same Kautz posted seven theses for debate on the door of a Worms church. These theses contained denials of predestination, satisfaction, and the Lutheran view of justification. The influence of Denck was apparent in them. Judging by Bucer's response, these theses, now lost, must have said something also about the issue of limited redemption. The rebuttal, issued in the name of the "Strassburg preachers" (which included Bucer), was directed by name against both Denck and Kautz, perceived together as a single threat to the gospel. This, the **Getrewe Warnung**,[2] contained frequent assertions of limited redemption[3] as well as a particularistic explanation of the universalistic texts used by Denck and Kautz.

The **Getrewe Warnung** did not silence the universal redemptionists in Strassburg. Pilgram Marpeck's **Confession of Faith** (1531) contained the doctrine that "Christ Jesus has through his blood taken away the sin of the whole world,"[4] by which he clearly meant every individual human being. In 1532, another Anabaptist preacher, Clemens Ziegler, accused Bucer of teaching limited redemption, saying that such a doctrine went against the clear meaning of John 11:51; this verse, perhaps not accidentally, would elicit one of Calvin's clearer comments on the extent of redemption.[5] Another preacher, Cornelius Poldermann, explained in 1534 that all men have been redeemed by Christ to the "first degree" of salvation, which is salvation from the "first death."[6] By this he meant that Christ redeemed all men without distinction to the extent that all men may now, if they so choose, believe and follow Christ. Not all, of course, do so. The death of Christ had

---

[1] Cf. **Quellen zur Geschichte der Täufer**, 14 vols. (Gütersloh: Gerd Mohn, 1930-), 7:60. Cf. Williams, p. 160.

[2] **Quellen**, 7:91-115.

[3] **Quellen**, 7:108, 107, 106.

[4] **Quellen**, 7:461.

[5] **Quellen**, 7:567.

[6] **Quellen**, 8:242.

for Poldermann, as it did for many of the Anabaptists, a function roughly parallel to the sacrament of baptism in Roman Catholic theology: to rescue man from the initial obstacle to his salvation (original sin; the "first death") and to place him in a position of neutrality where his own decisions, made with a free will that is the fruit of this general redemption, determine his final destiny.

Of all the Anabaptists, it was Melchior Hoffmann who proved most troublesome to Bucer, not least because Hoffmann's soteriology was in its central thrust a forerunner of Arminianism. He taught that God desires the salvation of every human being, loves every human being, and is in no sense the cause of evil or woe. That men perish is to be ascribed wholly to their own rejection of what God wants them to have.[1] God has opened the way to eternal life for all through Christ.[2] Hoffmann was not, as Denck appears to have been, a universal salvationist; hell and the wrath of God are vivid prospects for those who, in spite of God's proferred loved and salvation, persist in unbelief.

Between 1529 and 1533 Hoffmann was in and out of Strassburg and had several encounters with Bucer and the magistrates. In 1533 he appeared in the city for what would prove to be his last and permanent stay. The records of the Town Council indicate that it had already, in May 1533, perceived the challenge of Hoffmann to the prevailing doctrine of limited redemption. Hoffmann, said a report, taught that "God has created all men for blessedness, wants to damn no one, and Christ, the eternal Word of God, has died for us all, none excluded."[3] Partly because of this, he was a marked man. Then, in June 1533, the Strassburg Synod convened. Hoffmann was examined by it on two occasions. He presented some of the salient points of conflict between himself and the reformers in the form of five articles, the second of which asserted and defended universal redemption.[4] Christ, he said, died for all, none excluded, not for "half a world,"

---

[1] Quellen, 7:354-55.
[2] Quellen, 8:79.
[3] Quellen, 8:17.
[4] Quellen, 8:104-5.

but for the whole world and the whole seed of Adam.[1] For
Hoffmann, the biblical words "all" and "world" meant every human
being, and he accordingly adduced the same verses which had been
used for so long: I Cor. 15:22 ("As in Adam all die, so in Christ
shall all be made alive"), Rom. 5:18, I Tim. 2:4, I John 2:2, and
Rom. 11:32 ("that God might have mercy on all"). These passages
were still the heavy artillery of the universal redemptionist arsenal.

They were also still the passages which the limited
redemptionist had to explain, and Bucer set out to do so in July
1533 with a lengthy rebuttal of Hoffmann's five articles, the
Handlung gegen Hoffmann (Treatment Against Hoffmann). Bucer's
response to Hoffmann's second article was his most detailed
treatment of limited redemption, and included his exegeses of most
of the pertinent biblical passages from the other side. The **Getrewe
Warnung** of 1527 and the **Handlung gegen Hoffmann** were, taken
together, a pretty complete summary of Bucer's thought on the
particularity of redemption.

The fate of Hoffmann the universal redemptionist was similar
to that of Gottschalk the limited redemptionist, centuries earlier.
Following the Synod of Strassburg, he began an imprisonment that
would last until his death in 1543. Like Gottschalk, he was
troublesome to his captors even in captivity; the windows of his
cell eventually had to be sealed to prevent his preaching to the
people in the streets outside.

Hoffmann prophesied that Strassburg would be the site of the
New Jerusalem, but the effort to realize this prediction took place
instead, in grim form, in Münster. Still, the Münster Anabaptist
kingdom was in part Hoffmann's work since so many of its
inhabitants towards the end were Netherlanders to whom he had
preached and in whose minds he had instilled the hope of an
imminent coming of Christ. In this light it is no great surprise to
find a strong polemic against limited redemption in the work of
the Münster theologian, Bernhard Rothmann. Furthermore, it is
likely that Rothmann had spent time in Strassburg in the early
1530s and was well aware of the debate about limited redemption.
In the **Restitution** of 1534, Rothmann declared that part of the

[1] **Quellen**, 8:104-5.

pure doctrine being restored in Münster was the truth that Christ died for every human being. He used I Tim. 2:4, I John 2:2, and showed an awareness of the arguments of the opposing viewpoint.[1]

Thus far the historical setting. How did Bucer defend the concept of limited redemption?

Bucer's Defense of Limited Redemption

Bucer saw the nature of redemption and the extent of redemption as the warp and woof of one piece of cloth. In this respect his theology was very much like Gottschalk's. The concept of *satisfactio* was for Bucer central to the meaning of Christ's death; he saw Christ's sacrifice as above all a forensic event, a sacrifice for sins in the sight of God the Judge, and therefore objective and efficacious. As satisfaction, the death of Christ *was* redemption. The Anabaptists whose views have been preserved in the record of this strife with Bucer were quite uncomfortable with the concept of satisfaction, perhaps for the very reason that it led so logically to limited redemption: those for whom objective satisfaction has been made must be saved or God is unjust. Instead, the Anabaptists presented the death of Christ as the general work of God's grace which placed man in a salvable or redeemable state, and in a position where he is able to believe and follow Christ if he so chooses. It made salvation possible but not certain. To Bucer, this was nothing less than a denial of the gospel and of redemption. In his view the Anabaptist conception placed the final determination, and thus the burden, of salvation back on the shoulders of man and raised up the spectre of works-righteousness. It is interesting to observe that Bucer considered Michael Sattler, martyred in 1527, a "dear friend of God" and a "martyr of Christ"--this in spite of Sattler's anabaptism and rejection of the reformed view of the magistrate--on the ground that Sattler held that "faith alone saves."[2] This is an indication of what Bucer really considered central. And in his view Denck,

---

[1] **Restitution rechter christlicher Lehre**, cap. 5, **Die Schriften Bernhard Rothmanns**, ed. Robert Stupperich (Münster: Aschendorffsche Verlagsbuchhandlung, 1970), p. 231.
[2] **Quellen**, 7:110.

Kautz, and later Hoffmann were a different breed from Sattler
because their theology undercut the objective efficacy of
redemption and thus led back to works.

Another important feature of Bucer's doctrine of redemption
was its close connection to ethics. The radicals opposed the
particularism of the magisterial reformers not only because it
seemed to them to make God unjust, but because it appeared also
to destroy the motivation for discipleship. If salvation is entirely
a matter of God's work for man, they reasoned, does not
discipleship become a mere formality and the imperative of the
gospel lose its teeth? The radicals constantly complained that the
"Lutheran" gospel did nothing to change the lives of the people
who confessed it. In response to this critique, which Bucer felt
keenly, he set forth his own Augustinian conception of *Nachfolge*,
turning the Anabaptist logic upside down: where the Anabaptists
tended to make election and redemption depend on the proper
use of the will and obedience, Bucer made obedience dependent
on election and redemption, the subjective upon the objective.

> What nonsense it would be to say that Christ died for someone
> and made satisfaction, but that this person should not still have in
> him a Christian life! . . . For whom Christ made satisfaction,
> these will he cleanse and present to himself glorious.[1]

> Whoever knows fully and completely that the Father of our Lord
> Jesus Christ . . . is the only true God . . . and that our Lord Jesus
> is the only one who reconciles us to the Father and makes us his
> heirs, this person would of course want to desire and seek nothing
> else than God the Father through our Lord Jesus and to follow
> his word in all sincerity.[2]

While for the Anabaptist no discipleship was conceivable in the
vicinity of the doctrines of predestination and *satisfactio*, for Bucer
no discipleship was conceivable without them. The death of Christ
must be fruitful not only in the justification of the believer but
also in his sanctification. This insistence would also be

[1] **Quellen**, 7:106-7.
[2] **MBDS**, 5:76.

characteristic of Calvin. And it may well be that the Reformed tradition owed its strong emphasis on ethics, as conceived by Bucer and then by Calvin within the larger framework of the monergism of grace, to the proddings of the radicals. If so, it was to Bucer's credit that his reaction to the Anabaptist demand for an ethical life was, not to scoff at it as fanaticism (as Luther sometimes tended to do), but to respond to it in a constructive theological way. Whether this emphasis made any real difference in the moral tone of the Reformed cities and principalities is another question.

"Neither the election of God nor the redemption of Christ is common to all men," said Bucer to Hoffmann.[1] How then did he deal with the passages which Hoffmann and others brought against this doctrine?

Bucer accused the universal redemptionists of a basic linguistic blunder: they applied a standardized and predetermined meaning to the terms "all" and "world," one which ignored both biblical context and normal linguistic variety.[2] Theological predisposition dictated that for the universal redemptionist these terms must always mean *every* human being. That they can mean this, Bucer admitted; that they *must* mean this in every instance he denied.

And he illustrated his point. Sometimes in Scripture "all" simply means "many," that is, a group of people too large to number. When the Pharisees said, "The whole world runs after him [Christ]" (John 12:19), and, "All men will believe in him" (John 11:48), they obviously did not mean every human being without exception.[3] The context makes this clear.

Sometimes "all" is used when something is common to all men without distinction of kind.[4] Augustine's universalism of kinds was clearly recognizable here, and Bucer revealed his debt to Augustine by using one of his illustrations, the statement of Paul that he pleases "all men" (I Cor. 9:22). Augustine, it will be remembered, had also used homely similes from everyday life in

[1] MBDS, 5:78.
[2] MBDS, 5:83.
[3] MBDS, 5:83.
[4] MBDS, 5:83.

Hippo Regius; Bucer updated this technique and found one from his own civic situation:

> Here in Strassburg, where there is nothing special required to accept someone into citizenship, it is said: those in Strassburg accept everyone into citizenship, all men.[1]

This does not mean that every human being is a citizen of Strassburg, but that all kinds of human beings are citizens of Strassburg. Bucer utilized this universalism of kinds to exegete I Tim. 2:4 (more on this shortly) as well as to expound the statement of Jesus in John 17:2 that he has received authority "over all flesh." This means, said Bucer, that Christ has authority to save not merely Jews, but some from every kind of people. The result will be that the knowledge of salvation and the kingdom of God, previously limited to the confines of Judaism, will be dispersed over the whole earth.[2]

There is still another use of "all": "where something takes place or is given only through one person, so all who want to have such a thing must receive it from this one person."[3] This is Augustine's exclusive universalism. Again, in the "Handlung" Bucer lifted an illustration from Augustine and then created one of his own to go along with it: when it is said in common language that the mayor of Strassburg arrests, judges, and counsels all, this means, not that he does this to every person in the city, but that he is the one person in the city through whom these things are done.[4] Like Augustine, Bucer used this device to interpret Paul's parallel between Adam and Christ. "Just as no carnal generation is possible except through Adam, so no spiritual generation is possible except through Christ."[5] In Romans 5, the "many" who

[1] MBDS, 5:83.
[2] Enarrationes, p. 770.
[3] MBDS, 5:83.
[4] MBDS, 5:83.
[5] Metaphrases et enarrationes perpetuae epistolarum D. Pauli Apostoli . . . in Epistolam ad Romans . . . (Argentorati: VVendelinus Rihelius, 1536), p. 263.

die in Adam are actually *all*, and likewise the "many" who are made righteous in Christ are *all*. This is a significant instance of a limited redemptionist expanding "many" to "all"--Calvin would also take this approach (and Kendall would misunderstand him!). Yet Bucer explained that he was doing so only in terms of an exclusive universalism:

> And it is fitting to interpret this "many" as "all," since no one can obtain the mercy of God and life except through Christ.[1]

So, in this case, *many* means *all*, but *all* does not mean *every*.

Bucer also took over Augustine's two-worlds concept. When Christ says that his flesh gives "life to the world" (John 6:36-7), this means "all the elect, wherever they go among the nations." This is the world which God loved and for which he sent his Son (John 3:16). The other world is that which Jesus refers to when he says, "The world hates me" (John 15:18), and, "I pray not for the world" (John 17:9).[2] These verses had been standbys with Augustine. In the biblical statement that Christ is the "Lamb of God which takes away the sin of the world" (John 1:29), Bucer understood "world" to mean "all his own"[3] and that "which has been ordained to eternal life."[4]

The verses which had drawn forth Augustine's clearest explanations of limited redemption were treated similarly by Bucer. Denck and Kautz used Col. 1:19 ff., which speaks of Christ's reconciliation of all things in heaven and earth by his blood, to argue their position. But, Bucer replied, if their interpretation is correct, then even the devil himself must be reconciled, which is unthinkable. Rather, the passage means that "all the elect" are cleansed through Christ's blood,

> and St. Paul does not mention the devil, rather whatever is on earth and in heaven, by which he understands elect men and holy

---

[1] **Romans**, p. 160.
[2] **Enarrationes**, p. 671.
[3] **Enarrationes**, p. 589.
[4] **Quellen**, 7:461.

angels.[1]

Bucer also understood the "whole world" of I John 2:2 as a reference to the elect.[2] And the "all" whom Jesus draws to himself on the cross in John 12:32 are "all kinds of men."[3] References to I Tim. 2:4 in Bucer's writings reveal the same Augustinian pattern:

> And the scripture always pointed to, that God "wants all men to be saved and come to knowledge of the truth" (I Tim. 2:4), also applies only to the elect, but the elect of all peoples and tribes.[4]

> Certainly God has appointed his own people from all kinds and grades of men, whom he leads to the knowledge of the truth . . . That he says all is likewise as if he said, some from all, for there is no kind of man in which he does not have some of his own.[5]

While he limited "all" in this passage to the elect, Bucer was also careful to indicate that because we have no certain knowledge of the identity of the elect in this world, we must pray promiscuously for all, and specifically for those in authority, whom Paul mentions in the beginning of the passage.

Bucer's doctrine of limited redemption harked back to Augustine. There was hardly a trace of the complexity which had marked the scholastic discussions of this issue--Bucer made no mention of any secondary benefits of the death of Christ for the nonelect, nor did he distinguish antecedent and consequent wills of God or sufficient and efficient dimensions of Christ's sacrifice. The death of Christ was, quite plainly and unapologetically, only for the elect. The one real debt of Bucer to the medieval tradition after Augustine was the term *satisfactio*.

---

[1] **Quellen**, 7:114.
[2] **MBDS**, 5:85.
[3] **Enarrationes**, p. 733.
[4] **MBDS**, 5:85.
[5] **Enarrationes**, p. 169.

Bucer and Calvin

In Martin Bucer the limited redemptionist tradition was hand-delivered, as it were, to John Calvin.

Calvin's three years in Strassburg (1538-41) bore the imprint of Bucer's influence in many ways. In 1539 Calvin published a greatly expanded version of his already successful **Institutes** (1536), one that, according to F. Wendel, whose expertise encompassed both Calvin and Bucer, "betrays without any possible doubt an attentive reading of the Strassburg reformer."[1] The 1539 edition included a new and substantial section on predestination, and most scholars have seen here the imprint of Bucer's theology.[2] And Calvin openly acknowledged his debt to Bucer and his admiration for Bucer's skill as an exegete in regard to the latter's commentary on the gospels as well as his commentary on Romans, works from which we have drawn many of Bucer's limited redemptionistic statements.[3] So it is not necessary, though it is pleasant, to imagine long evening conversations by the light of oil lamps between the two men. Bucer's major theological works were available by 1536 in printed form.

This is not to suggest that Bucer was solely responsible for the content of Calvin's theology of predestination and related questions. It is probably more accurate to say that both Bucer and Calvin were indebted to Augustine, whose writings were of course available to Calvin quite independently of any relationship with Bucer. Nor is it to suggest that Calvin was a slavish follower of Bucer. It is striking testimony to Calvin's independence of judgment that he took issue, even in 1539, with Bucer's doctrine of the "seed of election" (that the elect display some signs of their

---

[1] François Wendel, **John Calvin: The Origins and Development of His Religious Thought,** trans. by Philip Mairet (London: Wm. Collins and Sons, 1963), p. 140.

[2] Both W. Pauck, *Calvin and Bucer,* **Journal of Religion,** 9 (1929):244, and A. Lang, *Martin Bucer,* **Evangelical Quarterly** 1 (April 1929):159, affirm the influence of Bucer's doctrine of predestination on Calvin.

[3] **Ioannis Calvini opera quae supersunt omnia,** 59 vols., ed. G. Baum, E. Cunitz, and E. Reuss (Brunswick and Berlin, 1863-1900), 45:4, 10(II):404. After this cited as **CO.**

election even before conversion).[1] He also gave a different analysis of the term "free will."[2]

The true significance of Calvin's contact with Bucer is that in the Strassburg reformation Calvin saw the old Augustinian soteriology in a specific historical context. The conflict of Bucer with the Anabaptists over the extent of redemption was no mere verbal squabble. For the Anabaptists, the death of Christ brought all men to the gate of heaven, but none into heaven. For Bucer, the death of Christ brought the elect, and none but the elect, into heaven. The chasm separating these two conceptions of the work of Christ was a wide one which touched the central nerve of the Christian gospel, and for that reason aroused considerable passion on both sides. Nor was Bucer alone on this point, since the other Strassburg preachers as well as the magistrates were of one mind in opposing the radical attack on limited redemption.[3]

What Calvin experienced, then, was a reformed city whose theology was limited redemptionist as well as predestinarian, a milieu in which limited redemption was used polemically against the threat from the radicals, and, most importantly, was perceived as part of the Reformation front against works-righteousness and Pelagianism. To put this in reverse: in the Strassburg context, the doctrine of universal redemption could not have appeared to Calvin in isolation, but rather in connection with the "Pelagianizing" gospel of the Anabaptists. Even in the late 1530s this was not a remote or forgotten matter, since the fright of the

---

[1] **Institutio Christianae Religionis** (1559) 3.24.10. Our citations from the **Institutes** are taken from **Joannis Calvini opera selecta**, vols. 3-5, ed. P. Barth and W. Niesel (München: D. Scheuner, 1926-52). The **Institutes** will be cited after this as **Inst.**

[2] Bucer, in the **Handlung** (**MBDS**, 5:79) tried to explain that *autexousias*, as used by the Greek fathers, referred simply to the spontaneity of human choice and not to fallen man's ability to choose good. He tried, in other words, to rescue the Greek fathers for Augustinianism.

[3] Both Capito and Hedio had a hand in the defense of limited redemption against the radicals. Cf. **Quellen**, 7:579, 8:190. In 1533 Bucer proposed limited redemption to Capito, Hedio, and Zell as one of the articles of faith to be adopted by the Strassburg Town Council, with the full assumption that they shared the same view. **Quellen**, 8:6.

Münster kingdom was still a recent memory, and poor Melchior Hoffmann still survived in his plastered-up cell as a reminder of the struggles through which the Strassburg reformation had come. If Bucer and Calvin did have any of those long evening talks, it is certain that they talked about Hoffmann.

In this environment Calvin would have read and thought about the extent of Christ's redemptive work. Human beings generally see ideas in clusters, in association with other ideas, and there is no reason to think that Calvin was an exception to this tendency. The Amyraut thesis maintains that Calvin held a doctrine which he surely knew to be the doctrine of men like Denck, Hoffmann, and Jan Bockelson the Anabaptist king of Münster, a doctrine which was regarded by his own reformed compatriots as an attack on the heart of the gospel, and against which the Strassburg reformation had taken a hard and public stand. Further, the Amyraut thesis implies that Calvin either misread Augustine on this point, or read him correctly and simply went a different way. While Calvin was ready to part ways with Augustine when necessary (as he did with Augustine's doctrine of infused righteousness), he did so where the whole magisterial Reformation parted ways with Augustine, and simply stuck with the Reformation "cluster" of ideas. But the Augustinian doctrine of limited redemption was part of the anti-Pelagian Augustine whom Calvin later claimed was "on our side."[1] The Amyraut thesis posits that Calvin was somehow able to surmount the tradition and the historical setting in which he stood, in one concrete and particular point, while retaining the rest of the package intact. It would be an astonishing thing. Whether it really happened will appear now, as we turn to Calvin himself.

[1] CO 8:266.

6

CHRIST AND ELECTION
IN CALVIN'S THEOLOGY

There is no single place where Calvin addressed the extent of Christ's redemption in a systematic fashion. The absence of such a *locus* in the **Institutes** has led some scholars to think that it was not important for him, but this was not the case. Calvin, unlike Bucer, was never much involved in controversies about the extent of redemption; like Augustine, his most significant statements are to be found in biblical exposition and preaching. This means for us that the evidence is strewn about, in the **Institutes** but also in the commentaries, the sermons, and the tracts, and I have attempted to gather together in a reasonably complete way Calvin's teaching that bears on our question. That is, above all, what needs to be done.[1]

But how to arrange the large body of evidence that emerges from Calvin's writings? Here the existence of the Amyraut thesis has tended to influence my approach. On the one hand, there is a body of evidence from the side of the Amyraut thesis, consisting of Calvin's statements about Christ's death for "all" and the "world," which needs to be evaluated. Advocates of the Amyraut thesis, as a matter of fact, have only scratched the surface here, especially in regard to Calvin's statements to the effect that souls perish for whom Christ died. To reach a valid conclusion about Calvin, it is essential to face this theological theme head-on, not simply to explain it away, but to account for its strong presence

---

[1] Treatments of Calvin's doctrine of election in its relationship to Christology can be found in Wilhelm Niesel, **The Theology of Calvin** (Philadelphia: Westminster Press, 1956); Paul Jacobs, **Prädestination und Verantwortlichkeit bei Calvin** (Clark, 1956); Wendel, **John Calvin**; and Muller, **Christ and the Decree.**

in Calvin's thought.

On the other hand, there is decisive evidence that Calvin was a limited redemptionist. Holding center stage in this group of evidence are Calvin's exegeses of the famous universalistic texts of the New Testament, John 12:32, I Timothy 2:4-6, I John 2:2, and the like. We have seen already how limited redemptionists from Augustine on handled these texts, and their importance in deciding the question was recognized by Kendall when he said that Calvin "generally leaves verses like these alone, but never does he explain, for example, that 'all' does not mean *all* or 'world' does not mean the *world*, as those after him tended to do."[1] This assertion of Kendall's was a huge mistake, and catastrophic for his whole case. As we shall see, in almost every case Calvin follows the Augustinian interpretation of the text.

The claims of the Amyraut thesis will also lead us beyond those Calvin passages that deal in some explicit way with the extent of redemption. It is claimed, for example, that Calvin maintained a universal saving will of God; that he did not link Christ's death to the decree of election, nor to Christ's work of intercession; that his doctrine of assurance was grounded in his doctrine of universal redemption. These claims take us beyond the proof-texts for or against limited redemption and demand a close look at some of Calvin's larger soteriological themes. It is with these that we begin.

Along the way we will hold Calvin's theology up against Amyraut's version of his theology (as expressed both by Amyraut and by his modern supporters), and find that the Saumur professor extensively distorted the reformer's thought.

The centrality of the death of Christ

As I worked through the Calvin *corpus*, I was, naturally, looking for Calvin's view of the extent of redemption. Other things came into focus too, things not so much looked for as felt by sheer repetition and accumulation. One of these things was that the center of Calvin's theology was Christ.

The "quest" for the center of Calvin's theology has yielded

---

[1] Kendall, p. 13, footnote 2.

other answers. Alexander Schweizer argued in the mid-nineteenth century that predestination was Calvin's *Centraldogma.*[1] This viewpoint has been repeated innumerable times since and has even passed into the popular consciousness. Certainly predestination was Calvin's dominant *polemical* topic.[2] Others have maintained that the doctrine of justification by faith alone formed the heart of Calvin's outlook.[3] There are good arguments for this contention as well, not least Calvin's own statement--certainly an echo of Luther's famous comment on justification as the article of the standing or falling church--that justification by faith alone is the "main hinge on which religion turns."[4]

But prominence must not be mistaken for centrality. Predestination and justification were extraordinarily important doctrines without which Calvin's theology would not be the same. Their prominence and frequency in his writings, however, was the special product of historical struggle. The deeper principle underlying both predestination and justification was for Calvin, as for the other magisterial reformers, that of *sola gratia.* Here was the chief treasure, the soul of the Reformation, and the heart of the gospel itself: salvation by God's grace alone, the radical reduction of man in his potentialities and abilities and the equally radical elevation of God in the sovereignty of his saving grace. Calvin perceived this principle to be under mortal assault, both from the side of Tridentine Catholicism with its affirmation of meritorious good works, to which Calvin counterposed justification *sola fide,* and from the side of the Anabaptists with their championing of free will, to which he counterposed predestination.

---

[1] Alexander Schweizer, **Die Protestantischen Centraldogmen in ihrer Entwicklung innerhalb der Reformierten Kirche,** 2 vols. (Zurich, 1854-56). This interpretation has been upheld more recently in David Wiley, *Calvin's Doctrine of Predestination: His Principal Soteriological and Polemical Doctrine* (Ph.D. dissertation, Duke University, 1971).

[2] For example, **Defensio sanae et orthodoxae doctrinae . . .** (1543), CO 6:225-404; **De aeterna Dei praedestinatione** (1552), CO 8:249-366; **Sur L'Election Eternelle** (1551), CO 8:85-118; **Brevis responsio Io. Calvini . . . ** (1557), CO 9:253-66; **De occulta dei providentia** (1558), CO 9:285-318.

[3] E.g. E. Doumergue, 4:267-71.

[4] Inst. 3.11.1.

The assaults on justification by faith alone and on predestination were for Calvin assaults on something that lay behind them in the theological holy of holies: the principle of grace. Salvation by grace was the treasure in the heart of the fortress, justification and predestination the outer bastions where most of the blood was spilled. Salvation by grace was the king on the chessboard, justification and predestination its queen and rooks.

But this still does not go deep enough. What does the abstract slogan *sola gratia* really embody? Calvin's answer to this, if I have absorbed anything at all from his writing and preaching, would be *Christ*. Simply Christ, incarnate, obedient, crucified, and risen. For what John Calvin really delighted to expound, lecture, and preach, when he was unencumbered with the burden of doing polemical battle with some enemy, was Christ. Christ, and the grace of Christ, is everywhere--in the commentaries, in the sermons, in the **Institutes** preeminently, in the Old Testament as well as the New, at the center of ethical instruction as well as soteriology, as much in the midst of the prayers of the Psalms as in the gospel narratives.[1]

Calvin was well aware of this Christological orientation of his thought, and often called attention to it explicitly. Especially did he focus in on the death and resurrection of Christ as the irreducible core of the gospel:

> For there is no part of our salvation which may not be found in Christ. By the sacrifice of his death he has purged our sins . . . by his resurrection he has purchased righteousness for us.[2]

[1] Richard Muller (**Christ and the Decrees**) proposed an alternative approach to the whole question of a "Centraldogma" in Calvin's theology. He refuted the notion that either Calvin or Reformed orthodoxy had a starting doctrine from which everything else was logically deduced, and argued that the central feature of Calvin's theology was actually the tandem (or the "multiple foci") of predestination and Christology. "The predestinarian structure (the decree and its execution) and the christological structure (the Son and his manifestation in the flesh) together provide a basis for the parallel development and mutual interpenetration of the doctrines of predestination and person of Christ." (p. 38)

[2] Comm. on Acts 20:21, **CO** 48:463.

The principal thing he did for our salvation was his death and
resurrection.[1]

Or even, at times, simply the death of Christ alone. In one place,
after an eloquent recitation of the benefits which the Messiah
would bestow--satisfaction for sin, reconciliation, righteousness,
regeneration--Calvin stated "that all those things were fulfilled in
the person of Jesus Christ crucified."[2] "We have in his death the
complete   fulfillment   of   our   salvation."[3]   "The   whole
accomplishment of our salvation, and all the parts of it, are
contained in his death."[4] "His sacrifice was the most important
part of his redemption."[5] The Christ of Calvin's gospel is the
Christ who is "never to be separated from his death."[6] The death
of Christ is his "principal office," and from "this source flow all
the streams of blessing."[7] If the death of Christ is seen this way,
it necessarily becomes the focal point of the believer's own
apprehension of salvation: "The whole assurance of life and
salvation rests upon the Lord's death."[8] Calvin could express this
all with a terse and paradoxical equation: "The death of Christ is
our life."[9]

It has not often been appreciated to what extent Calvin's
theology was a *theologia crucis*, not only as a soteriology but as
theology of the Christian life. There was in Calvin's thought, in a
way that must remind us strangely of the Anabaptists themselves,
the vision of the life of the church and the life of the individual
Christian lived under the humility of the cross.

Theological systems rooted in moralism or metaphysics could
conceivably bypass the question, for whom did Christ die? But

[1] Sermon on Acts 1:1-4, CO 48:586.
[2] Comm. on Acts 28:23, CO 48:569.
[3] Inst. 2.16.13.
[4] Comm. on John 19:30, CO 47:419.
[5] Comm. on Luke 24:26, CO 45:806.
[6] Comm. on Hebrews 9:22, CO 55:116.
[7] Comm. on John 1:29, CO 47:25.
[8] Inst. 4.17.37.
[9] Inst. 4.17.37.

Calvin's theology was a *theologia crucis*, with a *crux* on which the Redeemer saved men by suffering vicariously in their place. The death of Christ was, to be only a little hyperbolic, everything. So, to conclude, as a few historians have, that for Calvin the extent of redemption was a non-issue, is not only to be unaware of the history of the doctrine which we have traced (of which Calvin could not have been ignorant), but to say that Calvin did not think through his own most central tenet. Calvin had a position, which can be felt even as he speaks of the relationship of the Father and the Son in the work of salvation.

The work of the Father and the Son

If Calvin's theology was Christocentric, it was also Trinitarian. For Calvin, the eternal ontological unity of the Godhead was the premise of the work of salvation, so that the work of each person of the Godhead--whether Father, Son, or Spirit--is also the work of the whole Godhead; the classic orthodox doctrine of the Trinity is therefore closely reflected in the divine accomplishment of salvation.

> For this reason we obtain, and, so to speak, clearly discern in the Father the cause (*causa*), in the Son the substance (*materia*), and in the Spirit the effect (*effectus*) of our purgation and regeneration.[1]

Calvin in this remark borrowed the philosophical terminology of multiple causation to describe the unity-in-diversity of the work of the Trinity. This concept posits the most intimate kind of unity between the saving purpose of the Father and the saving work of the Son and Spirit. The particular interest of this study is with the relationship of the Father and the Son, and specifically with the question: in Calvin's thought, did the saving work of the Son correspond in scope and intention to the electing work of the Father?

To appreciate the importance of this topic it is necessary to return briefly to the theology of Moyse Amyraut, who believed

[1] Inst. 4.15.6.

that the will of the Father in regard to man's salvation was twofold. There was, first, a particular, predestinating, saving will of God directed toward the elect alone and effectuated through calling and the work of the Spirit. There was also a general saving will of God directed toward every human being and effectuated through the death of Christ and the general preaching of the gospel. Amyraut called these wills "covenants," respectively, the *foedus absolutum* and the *foedus hypotheticum*. The activity of God was a two-pronged thing with a clear division of labor between the Son, as the executor of one purpose, and the Spirit, as the executor of the other. Thus, in Amyraut's theology it was possible to say both, "God desires only the elect to be saved," and, "God desires every human being to be saved." Although Amyraut formally conceded that there must be some ultimate unity between these wills, he resisted the urge to reconcile them, preferring instead to emphasize the distinction and to leave them side by side. He summed it up well in these words:

> No, my brethren, when on the one hand the word of God will teach me that he has reprobated some and consigned them to eternal punishment, and that on the other hand this same word invites them to repent, that he extends his arms to them . . . although my reason found there some things which seemed to be in conflict, although whatever effort I exert I am not able to harmonize and reconcile them, still I will not fail to hold these two doctrines as true.[1]

The pivotal point in all this is that Amyraut linked the death of Christ to the general saving will of God and not to the electing will of God. The death of Christ was thus the effectuation of the *foedus hypotheticum*; it got its intention, its *telos*, from God's will to save every human being.[2] Then, that only the elect are actually saved was the result of the outworking of the *foedus absolutum*,

---

[1] Moyse Amyraut, **Sermons sur divers textes de la sainte ecriture.** 2nd ed. (Saumur: Desbordes, 1653). Armstrong's translation, p. 184.

[2] "La grace de la redemption qu'il leur a offerte et procurée deu estre egale et universelle." Amyraut, **Brief Traitté de la predestination et de ses principales dependances** (Saumur: J. Lesnier, 1634), p. 77.

effectuated by the Spirit. "The Spirit makes effective to the particular believer what Christ had accomplished for the world."[1]

Amyraut claimed Calvin in support of this conception, appealing to passages in which Calvin distinguished a "secret" and a "revealed" will of God,[2] and, of course, to passages in which Calvin taught that Christ died for "all" and for the "world." Amyraut was correct that there was in Calvin the identification of a revealed will of God by which God calls every man to salvation through the preached word. This doctrine of Calvin concerning the universal offer of the gospel will be examined more closely in another connection. The substructure of this teaching, however, for all its resemblance to that of Amyraut, was not the same. For Calvin was not content to be left with a double will of God. In the **Institutes** (1.18.3) he energetically argued that God's will is "one and simple," and explained its apparent duality not (as Amyraut) by appeal to two covenants in the eternal counsel of God, but to the imperfection of human perception.[3] While there may appear to humans to be two wills of God, in reality there are not. The duality of the divine will was for Calvin an epistemological thing; for Amyraut it assumed an ontological existence, to the extent that it could become for him a tool for the ordering of systematic theology.

The crucial question here is whether in Calvin's theology the saving work of Christ was linked to the particular saving purpose of God the Father. Amyraut said no; others, Kendall for instance, said no. But was Amyraut actually following Calvin? To come back to our earlier question, did the scope of the redemptive work of the Son correspond for Calvin to that of the electing work of the Father?

The answer must be yes. So identical in intention are the works of the Father and the Son that the term "Savior" is interchangeable between them:

The Father is called our Savior, because he redeemed us by the

[1] Armstrong, p. 177.
[2] **CO** 8:301; Comm. on II Peter 3:9, **CO** 55:476.
[3] Inst. 1.18.3.

death of his Son . . . and the Son, because he shed his blood as
the pledge and the price of our salvation. Thus the Son has
brought salvation to us from the Father, and the Father has
bestowed it through the Son.[1]

Both the Father and the Son are "Savior"; it may also be properly
said that each "gave himself" for us, though in different ways, the
Father by decreeing redemption from eternity and the Son by
carrying it out in history.[2]

This harmonious and connected work of the Father and the Son
had to do, in Calvin's theology, not with a general intention to
save every human being, but with the salvation of the elect. God's
saving will is at this point "one and simple"; it is directed toward
the elect, and is entrusted for its accomplishment (its *materia*, to
use the causal term) to Christ. At precisely this juncture in
Calvin's thought, the statement of Jesus, "All that the Father gives
me will come to me" (John 6:37), always an important text in the
discussions of predestination, became a central theme. Calvin
commented on the passage:

> Faith is not a thing which depends on the will of men, so that this
> man and that man indiscriminately and at random believe, but .
> . . God elects those whom he hands over, as it were, to his Son.[3]

This giving of souls by the Father to the Son is the language of
John's gospel for what Paul would call election, as Calvin
recognized. Whereas "election" and "predestination" denote mental
acts, "giving people to the Son" denotes a relational act; it draws
the Son into the act of election. Largely as a consequence of the
Johannine language, Christ became in Calvin's view the executive,
the trustee, of the election decree.

> Christ brings none to the Father but those given to him by the
> Father; and this donation, we know, depends on eternal election;
> for those whom the Father has destined to life, he delivers to the

---

[1] Comm. on Titus 1:3, **CO** 52:407.
[2] Comm. on Galatians 1:4, **CO** 50:170.
[3] Comm. on John 6:37, **CO** 47:146.

keeping of his Son, that he might defend them.[1]

The donation of the elect by the Father to the Son is thus a transaction rooted in predestination, and one that also faces the future; that Christ has been made the sole Protector of God's chosen people guarantees their final perseverance. We would surely perish

> were we not safe under the protection of Christ, whom the Father has given to be our guardian, so that none of those whom he has received under his care and shelter should perish.[2]

The Father gives the elect to the Son; the Son brings the elect to the Father; the Father wills their salvation and perseverance; the Son carries it out. All this was implied in Calvin's understanding of John 6:37, and because of the richness of the image and its appropriateness for the doctrine Calvin wanted to express, the picture of the Father entrusting the elect to Christ was an image that permeated his writing and preaching.

But where did the death of Christ, specifically, fit into this picture for Calvin? Did Christ, having received the elect as his peculiar donation from the Father, to bring them to the Father, to keep them and defend them, then proceed to give his life on the cross for every human being indiscriminately? It sounds strangely out of joint; but this is exactly what the Amyraut thesis asks that we believe about Calvin. The truth is otherwise.

"Let us therefore learn that every part of our salvation depends on [election]."[3] In Calvin's theology the free election of God was the source to which all other blessings of redemption must be traced. The dual involvement of Father and Son in election, implied in Calvin's teaching on John 6:37, suggests that Christ himself is an integral part of Calvin's doctrine of election. We turn now to an examination of Calvin's concept of the

---

[1] Comm. on Hebrews 2:13, **CO** 55:31.

[2] Comm. on Jude 1, **CO** 55:488. Cf. also **CO** 58:66.

[3] Comm. on John 13:18, **CO** 47:311. Election is understood here by the context.

relationship of Christ to election. Here we will identify four themes: that Christ is the elector; that election is in Christ; that Christ is the executor of election; and that the assurance of election is to be found in Christ.

Christ the elector

Calvin never lost sight of the fact that Christ, who for the salvation of men took to himself a human nature and became thereby the Mediator between God and men, nevertheless preexisted as the fully divine and sovereign second person of the Trinity. "Unchangeable, the Word [i.e. the Son] abides everlastingly one and the same with God, and is God himself."[1] Here again was Calvin's premise that the persons of the Trinity operate in unity; as eternal God, the Son necessarily participated in the decree of election.

> Meanwhile, although Christ interposes himself as Mediator, he claims for himself, in common with the Father, the right to choose . . . From this we may infer that none excel by their own effort or diligence, seeing that Christ makes himself the author of election (*electionis authorem*).[2]

The right of Christ to designate himself as the *author electionis* rests, not only upon his own personal authority as Deity, but upon the intimate sharing of function which exists between the Father and the Son, a kind of *communicatio officiarum*:

> That Christ declares himself to be the author of both [election and ordination] is not to be wondered at, since it is only by him that the Father acts, and he acts with the Father. So then, both election and ordination belong equally to both.[3]

So while it was Calvin's usual pattern of thought to ascribe election to God the Father, he could also on occasion speak of

[1] **Inst.** 1.13.7.
[2] **Inst.** 3.22.7. Cf. also **CO** 47:311.
[3] Comm. on John 15:16, **CO** 47:347.

Christ as the one who "has chosen and set apart the church as his bride,"[1] and of the church as elected by Christ.[2] These references to Christ as *author electionis*, while not numerous, were direct and clear. While Calvin normally saw Christ in his servant-mediator role, he never forgot that Christ did not cease to be God, even in his incarnation.

Election in Christ

The complexity of Calvin's thought concerning the relationship of Christ to election begins to appear even more clearly in his concept of Christ as the *locus* of election, or the one in whom election takes place. In this role Christ stands, not as the one facing man and acting sovereignly upon him, but as the Mediator standing alongside his people as they are considered by God as objects of his election.

The passage Ephesians 1:4 ("[God] chose us in him before the foundation of the world.") exercised an enormous influence on Calvin, as it had on predestinarians before him; it furnished him not only with a prooftext for the doctrine of election, but also with a Christological connection: "in him." Calvin derived from these words the principle that the union of the redeemed with Christ began "before the foundation of the world." He used this idea to push Christology back into election: Christ did not begin to function as mediator only at his incarnation, but was present and involved when the elective decree of God was made.

This doctrine suffused Calvin's writing and preaching. In the short space of one paragraph of a sermon on Esau and Jacob, he said: "God chose us before the creation of the world in Jesus Christ . . . St. Paul says that he chose us in Jesus Christ . . . Our election is founded in Jesus Christ."[3]

What did Calvin mean by this? He meant that in the act of

---

[1] **Inst.** 4.1.10.

[2] Comm. on Luke 8:2, **CO** 45:356.

[3] Sermon on Genesis 25:19-22, **CO** 58:49. Calvin's Christological concept of election was in line with Bucer's. In his comments on Ephesians, Bucer stressed that election is "through Christ," and "in Christ," and is enacted only "by the merit of Christ's blood." Cf. Stephens, p. 25.

election God regarded those whom he chose, not as they were in themselves (that is, as they would be when they were created), but as they were (or would be!) in union with Jesus Christ. It was, one might say, a matter of how God graciously chose to perceive his elect. Given this, certain things followed for Calvin.

First, election in Christ meant for Calvin that human merit was excluded, not only in the course of the individual's historical life, not only at conception and birth, but at the absolute fountainhead of salvation in the decree of God. This was Calvin's comment on Eph. 1:4:

> "In Christ." This is the second proof that the election was free; for if we were chosen in Christ, it is not of ourselves. It is not from a perception of anything that we deserve, but because our heavenly Father has introduced us, through the privilege of adoption, into the body of Christ. In short, the name of Christ excludes all merit, and everything which men have of their own; for when he says that we are chosen in Christ, it follows that in ourselves we are unworthy.[1]

This is one of the arguments with which Calvin countered the notion, urged by his antipredestinarian opponents, that election was based upon God's foreknowledge of something the individual would do as the condition for the bestowal of grace. Calvin argued that if this were the case, there would be no need for God to elect us *in Christ*. The intervention of Christ even at the point of divine election therefore excludes merit.

> Those whom God has adopted as his sons are said to have been chosen not in themselves but in his Christ; for unless he could love them in him, he could not honor them with the inheritance of his kingdom.[2]

---

[1] Comm. on Eph. 1:4, **CO** 51:147. Cf. also **CO** 51:269, where Calvin called Christ *le vray registre* of election.

[2] **Inst.** 3.24.5.

Now if they are elect in Christ, it follows that . . . each man is elected without respect to his own person.[1]

The doctrine of election in Christ also functioned in Calvin's theology to buttress the doctrine of perseverance, the endurance of the elect to the end in faith. Much more than a stark divine decree, election defined in this Christocentric way is the creation of an indissoluble personal bond, very much like a marriage, between Christ and the elect. To describe this elective union Calvin resorted habitually to the Pauline image of Christ as the "head" of his "members":

We must, in order that election may be effectual and truly enduring, ascend to the head, in whom the heavenly Father has gathered his elect together and has joined them to himself by an indissoluble bond.[2]

This redemptive organism of head and members, once created, can never be torn asunder; therefore the effectuation of election is certain. The "members of Christ," once "ingrafted to their head," are "never cut off from salvation."[3]

As a result of this, the doctrine of election in Christ meant for Calvin that the whole weight of the believer's assurance of his own election must rest on Christ. If the effectuation of election flows from head to members, then the members must always look to the head. This leads us logically to the topic of assurance, which, as we will shortly see, was for Calvin Christocentric.

Calvin's doctrine of election in Christ, and particularly his insistence that God's consideration of the elect in Christ excludes merit, brings up a form of the cart-and-the-horse question: if God saw the elect in Christ as he elected them, then how did they come to be in Christ in the first place? Was election the act of God's *placing* humans in Christ, or was it--as the recently quoted statements would suggest--the act of God's *seeing* the elect already

[1] Inst. 3.22.2.
[2] Inst. 3.21.7.
[3] Inst. 3.21.7.

in Christ and setting their destiny? Calvin was not unaware of this question, and addressed it directly:

> Although we are elected in Christ, still in terms of order God's considering us as among his own people is first, and his making us members of Christ is second.[1]

God's determination to save came first in terms of logical order, and his determination to save through union with Christ came second. Yet both, taken together as a unity, constituted election for Calvin. Election was, to revert to the language of John 6:37, the act by which God the Father handed over a people to the Son.[2]

Christ the executor of election

Was the Christ who was himself the elector, and in whom election took place, also for Calvin the one who carried out the decree of election by his own redemptive work? This is the most important question we have posed so far. For the Amyraut thesis *must* say no to this. If Christ is the executor of election, then his death, as the centerpiece of his work, must be for the elect.

F. Wendel affirmed that Calvin saw Christ as the executor of election.[3] R. T. Kendall, however, denied this: "The decree of election, however, is not [for Calvin] rendered effectual by the death of Christ."[4] Kendall was at this point fighting for the life of his thesis about Calvin; he realized that if Christ was the executor of election through his death, limited redemption follows as a consequence. But the texts support Wendel.

---

[1] CO 9:714.

[2] Perhaps it is here, in connection with the topic of election in Christ, that we should mention Calvin's reference to Christ as the *object* of election. This comment (**Inst.** 2.17.1) was wholly dependent on Augustine (**De praedestinatione sanctorum liber, MPL** 44:981). Since Calvin used the idea only here, and that for a special polemical purpose, it should not be considered a major element of his view of election and Christ.

[3] F. Wendel, **Calvin**, pp. 231-2.

[4] Kendall, p. 15.

A third time he repeats that the decree was eternal and unchangeable, but that it must be ratified by Christ, because in him it was made.[1]

The mediatorial work of Christ is that means by which God's decree was ratified (*sanciri*). And Calvin rooted this arrangement in the fact that the decree of election took place "in him." An election which took place *in* Christ is most fittingly carried out *by* Christ. Again, the same doctrine:

[Christ] has been manifested to the world in order to ratify (*ratum faciat*) by his own work (*ipso effectu*) what the Father has decreed concerning our salvation.[2]

For, by the coming of Christ, God executed what he had decreed.[3]

Because it was through the Mediator that God "ratifies" and "executes" his eternal decree,[4] Christ was the "channel" (*canalis*) through whom our salvation, eternally hidden in the predestination of God, flows to us.[5] And the nexus between election and the mediatorial work of Christ can be described as that between a plan and its fulfillment.[6]

Election, important as it was for Calvin, was in itself an empty act, ineffectual for the salvation of men, if not ratified and executed. Christ is the one who did this by his redemptive work. The eternal covenant of adoption, made with the elect, must be made firm "through the hand of Christ (*per manum Christi*)."[7]

Calvin made a parallel point when he spoke of Christ as the one through whom the secret purpose of God was revealed. The emphasis here was not effectuation but manifestation. God's

[1] Comm. on Eph. 3:11, **CO** 51:183.
[2] Comm. on John 6:38, **CO** 47:146.
[3] Comm. on I Peter 1:20, **CO** 55:226.
[4] Comm. on John 6:40, **CO** 47:147.
[5] Comm. on Matt. 11:27, **CO** 45:319.
[6] Sermon on II Timothy 1:9-10, **CO** 54:54.
[7] **Inst.** 2.6.4.

hidden purpose was made "clear and manifest" by the appearance of Christ.[1] "The predestination of God is in itself hidden, but it is manifested to us in Christ alone."[2] The same nexus between the work of Christ and election underlies this theme. And because the manifestation of Christ in human history was the revelation of election, Christ becomes, again from this new angle, the focal point of assurance.

Yet another path into Calvin's thought on the relationship of election to Christ is his doctrine of the love of God. There was for Calvin a sense in which God "loves" all his creatures, including even the reprobate, but this love amounts in the final analysis to God's present patience with them and his bestowal upon them of many temporal blessings before the final judgment day. This concept was not akin to Wyclif's idea of "secondary benefits" of redemption; Calvin never connected the idea to the sacrifice of Christ. In this connection we might also mention that there was no trace in Calvin's theology of the idea, often ascribed to him, that worldly prosperity is a visible sign of election. God causes the rain to fall on the unjust as well as the just (Matt. 5:45). This universal "love" of God is then a kind of universal benevolence.[3] But it is not the soteriological love of the gospel which issues in the redemption and renewal of sinners. Calvin reserved the love of God in this sense for the elect alone. His salvific love is directed to "his elect"[4] and to "the whole church."[5] And the following statement is blunt: "God embraces in fatherly love none but his children."[6]

God's love in this sense was for Calvin synonymous with election. Here again the Ephesians 1 passage had a formative role in Calvin's thought since it designates the divine love as the motive for God's predestination of the elect (1:5). So Calvin often intertwined the themes of election before the beginning of time

---

[1] Sermon on II Tim. 1:9-10, **CO** 54:59.
[2] Comm. on John 17:6, **CO** 47:379.
[3] Comm. on Mark 10:21, **CO** 45:541.
[4] Comm. on John 17:24, **CO** 47:390.
[5] Comm. on Matt. 12:18, **CO** 45:331.
[6] Comm. on Mark 10:21, **CO** 45:540.

and God's love. The Father's favor is "the love with which God embraced us before the foundation of the world,"[1] and the elect are "those whom he loved before the creation of the world."[2] Furthermore, God's love, like his election (or, perhaps more accurately, because love and election are simply two aspects of the same divine act), is *in Christ*. Christ is the person in whom the elect are loved;[3] since sinners are inherently odious to God, it is necessary that God love them in the acceptability and merit of Christ, the Beloved Son.

Finally--and in this sense too Calvin's doctrine of God's love resembled his doctrine of election--God's love was expressed and effectuated through the redemptive work of Christ. He is, said Calvin, the "mirror" of God's love.[4] The love of the Father for his children cannot remain a mere sentiment; it must take expression in redeeming action.

> For how comes it that we are saved? It is because the Father loved us in such a manner that he determined to redeem and save us through the Son.[5]

The redemption which the Father effected through the Son was, then, the outworking of his special love for the elect. Calvin captured something of the New Testament linkage of the divine love with the divine gift which appears in passages like John 3:16 ("God so loved the world that he gave . . . "), Galatians 2:20 ("the Son of God, who loved me and gave himself for me"), and Ephesians 5:25 ("Christ loved the church and gave himself for her"). God loved and so he gave, and the giving of which these passages speak is specifically the giving of Christ in his sacrificial death; following this pattern, Calvin coupled God's love with the death of Christ:

---

[1] Inst. 2.16.4.
[2] Inst. 2.17.2.
[3] Cf. **CO** 45:540-41, 47:390.
[4] Inst. 2.12.4.
[5] Comm. on I Tim. 1:1, **CO** 52:249.

How did God begin to embrace with his favor those whom he had
loved before the creation of the world? Only in that he revealed
his love when he was reconciled to us by Christ's blood.[1]

The love with which God embraced us before the creation of the
world was established and grounded in Christ. These things are
plain and in agreement with scripture, and beautifully harmonize
those passages in which it is said that God declared his love
toward us in giving his only begotten Son to die (John 3,16).[2]

The sense of these passages is that Christ's death is the
revelation and effectuation of God's love for the elect.

According to Calvin, Christ was the executor of election. He
was also, and specifically in his death, the manifestation and
effectuation of the love of God for the elect. Surely, as even
Kendall recognized, the logical outcome of such a Christology is
the doctrine of limited redemption.[3]

Christ and the assurance of election

The role of Christ in the believer's assurance was a dominant
theme for Calvin. R. T. Kendall claimed that Calvin's
Christocentric doctrine of assurance, based on universal
redemption, was replaced in the "experimental predestinarian"
theology of the English Calvinists by an introspective mode of
assurance; he claimed that this change was the result of the
introduction of the idea of limited redemption through Beza.
"Beza's doctrine inhibits the believer from looking directly to
Christ's death for assurance," he stated.[4] "Had Christ died for all,
we could freely know that we are elected," he asserted; however,
because of limited redemption, assurance "must be sought
elsewhere than in Christ."[5] This contention needs to be tested
against Calvin's own exposition of Christ's role in assurance.

Calvin's doctrine of assurance was bordered by two premises

---

[1] Cf. **Inst.** 2.16.4.
[2] **Inst.** 2.16.4.
[3] Kendall, p. 15.
[4] Kendall, p. 29.
[5] Kendall, p. 32.

which, like the banks of a river, determined its direction and shape. On the one side lay the fact that election is secret. Calvin often reminded his hearers and readers that God's predestination, considered in itself, is inscrutable and inaccessible to human knowledge. He described election characteristically as "secret" or "hidden." As he began his treatment of election in the **Institutes**, he warned that those who presumptuously rush into this doctrine in order to satisfy their own curiosity will find themselves in a labyrinth.[1] Philosophical and speculative inquiries into election are ruled out. There is absolutely nothing man can do to discover his election.

On the other side lay the necessity to know one's own election. Such knowledge Calvin considered essential for spiritual health. He took a staunch stand, as a Reformation theologian, against the medieval doctrine of uncertainty which was formulated emphatically at Trent. He said, "Satan has no more grievous or dangerous temptation to dishearten believers than when he unsettles them with doubt about their election."[2] He considered it no part of piety or humility to be in doubt about one's own election. Rather, piety was, for Calvin, to be certain of it and therefore to be able to ascribe the praise for such grace to God with a confident heart. True piety flows from certainty.

So the question arises: how does the believer know something which must be known but which cannot be known through direct knowledge? Calvin asked this question himself: "What revelation do you have of your election?"[3] The word "revelation" is crucial here; it signals one of Calvin's important assumptions. If there is to be any knowledge of election, it will have to be because God reveals it, not because man has found it out in an empirical manner. But Calvin had good news: God does in fact reveal to the believer the knowledge of his election.

How? Calvin's answer to his own question was multilayered. The believer's calling--the awakening of faith which is the work of the Holy Spirit through the gospel--is incontestable evidence of

[1] Inst. 3.21.1.
[2] Inst. 3.24.4.
[3] Inst. 3.24.4.

election,[1] since "those whom he predestined, he also called" (Rom. 8:29). Knowledge of election is also to be sought and found only in the word.[2] But in the end it is Christ himself on whom Calvin focused his doctrine of the assurance of election. For it is Christ whom the word reveals, and it is Christ to whom the elect person is drawn through calling. To push through the implications of Calvin's theology is to find oneself again and again, and from every possible angle, face to face with Christ.

> We must always come to our Lord Jesus Christ when it is a question of our election.[3]

> How do we know that God has elected us before the foundation of the world? By believing in Jesus Christ.[4]

> Do you want then to know that you are elect? Consider yourself in Jesus Christ.[5]

Only by founding the assurance of election on Christ can the believer avoid despair on the one hand and the quagmire of speculative investigation of God's unsearchable mind on the other. Certainty of election is through Christ alone, and all who inquire into it by any other means are "insane to their own destruction."[6]

Building on this Christocentric foundation, Calvin employed a rich variety of verbal images to express the place of Christ in the assurance of election. To apprehend God's election, faith directs itself to Christ, who is the "pledge of election" (*electionis arram*).[7] Christ, that is, can be likened to the down payment or

---

[1] Inst. 3.24.4.

[2] Inst. 3.21.2.

[3] Sermon on II Tim. 1:9-10, **CO** 54:58.

[4] Sermon on Eph. 1:4-6, **CO** 51:281.

[5] **Sur L'Election Eternelle, CO** 8:114.

[6] Comm. on I John 4:10, **CO** 55:353-54.

[7] Comm. on Acts 13:48, **CO** 48:314. The Latin *arrha* and its closely related synonym *arrhabo* appear to be borrowed from the Greek *arrabon*, which Paul uses in II Cor. 1:22, 5:5, and Eph. 1:4 to characterize the work of the Spirit. The application of the term to Christ is Calvin's own idea.

earnest money which proves the good faith of the giver and is in fact a portion of that which has been promised. The gospel, when received by believers, is an "authentic letter"--a faithful and trustworthy copy of the original document--of their election, because it is "signed" by the blood of Christ.[1] Calvin also refers to Christ's blood as a "sacred seal" (*sacrosanctum sigillum*) which erases the doubt that so often assails the believer.[2]

So Christ was for Calvin the pledge, the notarized copy, and the sacred seal of election. But the most important and common of Calvin's analogies was that of Christ as the "mirror" (*speculum*) of election. This image, as the following passage from the **Institutes** shows, was grounded in the concept of election in Christ. If election was in Christ, reasoned Calvin, then it is only in Christ that assurance may be found.

> But if we have been chosen in him, we shall not find assurance of our election in ourselves; and not even in God the Father, if we conceive him as severed from his Son. Christ, then, is the mirror wherein we must, and without self-deception may, contemplate our own election.[3]

The same analogy occurred frequently in the sermons,[4] once with a striking double vantage point: not only is Christ the mirror in which we behold our election, but also the mirror in which God beholds us to find us acceptable.[5] There was for Calvin, it would seem, no direct relationship between the Father and his elect. Christ stands always between.

But what did it mean that Christ is *speculum electionis*? To answer this it is possible to draw on a wealth of references to *speculum* and *miroir* in Calvin's writings to form a definition. Indeed, to read the Calvin *corpus* at any length is to be struck by how often the term comes up. In a few cases, Calvin used "mirror"

---

[1] Sermon on II Tim. 1:9-10, **CO** 54:57.
[2] Comm. on I Tim. 6:13, **CO** 52:330.
[3] **Inst.** 3.24.5.
[4] Sermon on II Tim. 1:9-10, **CO** 54:54.
[5] Sermon on Eph. 1:4-6, **CO** 51:281-82. Cf. also **CO** 51:269.

in a way that was roughly equivalent to "example": the history of the church in Acts is a mirror of perseverance in tribulation,[1] and the godly family described by Paul in Titus is a mirror of chaste behavior.[2] But this was not the typical meaning. Almost always it had a deeper sense. The "mirror" in Calvin's mind was a symbolic or even a typological thing, a bearer of meaning beyond itself in which a more profound or general truth may be glimpsed. The Old Testament types, Calvin said, were mirrors of heavenly reality;[3] man is a mirror of God's glory;[4] the word is a mirror of God himself;[5] David is a mirror of Christ,[6] Jacob of the whole church of the elect,[7] nature of the glory of God,[8] and the Lord's Supper of Christ's death.[9] The physical creation, redemptive history, and the Scripture itself formed for Calvin a complex revelatory structure through which God, who is always fundamentally *deus absconditus*, wills to reveal himself. The mirrors are the vehicles of this revelation. Through them man learns about the true God in indirect ways. The knowledge of God for Calvin was always this kind of mirror-knowledge, true but indirect.

Christ himself was the mirror *par excellence*. In the person of Christ the necessity of prying into the secrets of heaven is obviated, for in his face the God who would otherwise be hidden and distant appears.[10] Christ is the mirror of God's grace,[11] of God's love,[12] of all ethical perfection,[13] and therefore of Christian

---

[1] Comm. on Acts 16:11, **CO** 48:375.
[2] Comm. on Titus 1:16, **CO** 52:410.
[3] **Inst.** 2.11.1.
[4] **Inst.** 2.12.6.
[5] **Inst.** 3.2.6.
[6] Sermon on Matt. 26:40-50, **CO** 46:854.
[7] Sermon on Gen. 27:11-19, **CO** 58:174.
[8] Sermon on II Thess. 1:6-10, **CO** 52:230.
[9] Comm. on Matt. 26:29, **CO** 45:709.
[10] Comm. on John 5:22, **CO** 47:114.
[11] Comm. on Eph. 1:20, **CO** 51:158.
[12] Comm. on John 15:9, **CO** 47:342.
[13] Sermon on Matt. 27:11-26, **CO** 46:900.

conduct.[1] He stands at the very center of the revelatory structure of God. To see and to understand the Mediator is for Calvin to see and understand God, indirectly but truly.

This is the larger context of Calvin's references to Christ as the *speculum electionis*. The image is not poetic or allusive, but precise and theological. It meant in Calvin's usage that Christ is the point at which God's election pierces, as it were, through the cloud of secrecy in which God's decree is normally veiled. To behold Christ in faith is to behold one's own election. Beyond Christ it is not only unnecessary but unlawful to pry to find certainty of election. And the Christ who, seen with faith, is the mirror of election was undoubtedly for Calvin Christ crucified: "Therefore, whenever our hearts waver, let us remember that we should always go to the death of Christ for confirmation."[2] Because the election of God is revealed in the death of Christ, believers may find assurance at the cross.

The figure of Christ the Mediator loomed over the landscape of Calvin's doctrine of election like a mountain. There was literally no doctrine of election without him. He was there, at the making of the decree of election, as its co-author. He was there also as the one in whom election took place, covering the elect already, in the divine counsel, with his merit. He undertook, in history, as the incarnate God, to execute and reveal the decree of election by his life, death, and resurrection. He presents himself, through the word, as the anchor of assurance.

This all points logically to the doctrine of limited redemption. If Christ elected his people, it would seem to follow that it was for them he died. If Christ was the executor of election, it would seem to follow that his task was to redeem the elect. There was no trace in Calvin's theology of the doctrine attributed to him by Amyraut, that Christ came to carry out something other than the predestinating decree of God for the salvation of the elect. Everywhere Calvin's doctrine was that Christ's redemptive work was linked to, flowed from, and carried out the election of God.

What about Kendall's claim that Puritanism lost Calvin's

[1] Comm. on Philippians 2:9, **CO** 52:28.
[2] Comm. on I Tim. 6:13, **CO** 52:330.

doctrine of assurance because of limited redemption? On a theological level the sense of this is not clear. How can a Christ who died for everyone, even the nonelect who will perish, be a source of the assurance of election? Kendall misread both the mind and the heart of the predestinarians who advocated limited redemption. If anything is clear in theologians like Beza, Perkins, and Whitaker--whom Kendall treated--it is that limited redemption was for them *precisely a doctrine of assurance.*[1] Kendall was convinced that only a universal redemption can bring assurance to be focused on Christ. But the limited redemptionists were convinced that only a limited redemption can accomplish this. For, as they argued, if Christ died for everyone but only the elect will be saved, then there are humans for whom Christ died but who will perish anyway. So it does the troubled soul no good to know that Christ died for him; he may be "redeemed" but still on his way to hell. He still does not know if he is elect. The Puritans argued that only when the scope and intention of Christ's work corresponds to that of the Father's election does Christ function meaningfully in assurance. If I know that Christ died for me (which knowledge is, in Calvinism, imparted by the testimony of the Spirit), then I know, without further probing or speculation, that I am elect. And this is exactly what Calvin himself meant by calling Christ the "mirror of election."

---

[1] Dewey Wallace noted the proper emphasis of the doctrine of limited redemption in Puritan theology in **Puritans and Predestination** (Chapel Hill: University of North Carolina Press, 1982), p. 48.

7

CHRIST'S DEATH AND CALVIN'S LARGER SOTERIOLOGY

In this chapter we will continue to explore Calvin's understanding of Christ's death in its relationship to other aspects of his theology, especially to several soteriological themes.

The Death of Christ and the Causes of Salvation

In Amyraut's theology, God worked along two distinct paths generated by the *foedus absolutum* and the *foedus hypotheticum*: along the path of the former lay election and the regenerating work of the Spirit in the elect, along the latter lay the death of Christ for every human being and the universal call of the gospel. Christ's death was not theologically connected to election.

Amyraut claimed Calvin for this, but he was wrong. Calvin saw God's saving work proceeding along one straight, integrated path. Nowhere did this come to more compact and systematic expression than in his exposition of the "causes" of salvation. We have already encountered this conception in Calvin's statement that the Father is the cause (*causa*), the Son the substance (*materia*), and the Spirit the effect (*effectus*) of our salvation[1]. In this chapter we will explore Calvin's use of this causation scheme in more detail.

It is at this point in his theology that we meet the reformer in his most "scholastic" mode. Without any hesitation or self-consciousness, Calvin adopted the Aristotelian architectonic device of fourfold causation to describe his concept of the unity of salvation. This appeared first in the year 1539, in both the second

---

[1] **Inst.** 4.15.6.

edition of the **Institutes** and the commentary on Romans.[1] In both cases it was the interpretation of Romans 3:23-25 which led Calvin to comment on the theme of causation. This occurred, it should be noted, early in his career, and at a time when he had come most strongly under the influence of Bucer, who also used the concept of causation in a similar way.[2] Calvin's explanation in the **Institutes** was as follows:

> The philosophers postulate four kinds of causes to be observed in the outworking of things. If we look at these, however, we will find that, as far as the establishment of our salvation is concerned, none of them has anything to do with works. For Scripture everywhere proclaims that the efficient cause (*efficientem causam*) of our obtaining eternal life is the mercy of the heavenly Father and his freely given love to us. Surely the material cause (*materialem*) is Christ, with his obedience, through which he acquired righteousness for us. And what shall we say is the formal or instrumental cause (*formalem vel instrumentalem*) but faith? As for the final cause (*finalem*) the apostle testifies that it consists both in the proof of divine justice and in the praise of God's goodness.[3]

Having defined these four causes, Calvin then adduced Romans 3:23-25 as an example, and found here the "primal source" (efficient cause) in God's mercy, the material cause in Christ's

---

[1] David N. Wiley believed that the concept of multiple causation was implicit even in the earliest edition of the **Institutes** (1536), although the technical terminology was not yet used (*Calvin's Doctrine of Predestination*).

[2] Bucer, for example, did this in his commentary on Ephesians 1. "Huius causam efficientiem dicit esse meram gratiam Dei, et meritum Christi . . . Causae finales sunt, vitae sanctificatio, et gloria Dei." **Praelectiones doctiss. in epistolam D. P. ad Ephesios, eximij doctoris D. Martini Buceri . . .** (1562), p. 19. He also did so in his comments on Romans 3, where he identified the *prima causa* as the goodness of God, the *proxima causa* as Christ, and other intermediary causes as various kinds of people (e.g. parents, elders) and good works (understood as the gift of God). The fact that Calvin's use of the *causa* theme came in connection with these same passages is strong proof of the influence of Bucer.

[3] **Inst.** 3.14.17.

righteousness, the instrumental cause in faith, and the final cause in the demonstration of God's righteousness. In the Romans commentary of the same year the passage was interpreted in the same way.[1]

The scheme of fourfold causation, once introduced in these 1539 writings, was one which Calvin utilized often thereafter. Following Bucer, he found the tool a helpful one in the exegesis of Ephesians 1 (1548):

> Three causes of our salvation are here mentioned and a fourth is shortly afterward added. The efficient cause is the good pleasure of the will of God, the material cause is Jesus Christ, and the final cause is the praise of his grace.[2]

The formal cause, he noted when he came to v. 8, is the preaching of the gospel. Much later, in 1560, Calvin reverted to the same structure in his comment on Acts 22:16:

> Therefore, when the question is one of the remission of sins, we must seek no other author thereof but the heavenly Father, we must imagine no other material cause but the blood of Christ; and when we come to the formal cause, the Holy Spirit is the main one. But there is an inferior instrument, and that is the preaching of the word and baptism.[3]

In this passage Calvin integrated the causation scheme with the doctrine of Trinitarian salvation: the first three causes are the Father, the Son, and the Spirit, and the fourth is for this reason called "inferior." This is a systematic theologian at work!

So far we have seen passages where Calvin grouped the causes together. Far more common are references to the causes separately, as Calvin encountered the various aspects of salvation. Election is the "first cause,"[4] the cause which itself has no causes,[5]

---

[1] Comm. on Romans 3:22-24, **CO** 49:60.
[2] Comm. on Eph. 1:5, **CO** 51:148.
[3] Comm. on Acts 22:16, **CO** 48:496.
[4] **CO** 48:61, 49:159.
[5] **CO** 54:48.

and the "highest cause" of our salvation and all its parts.[1] Jesus Christ, said Calvin, is the "second cause" of life,[2] the cause of salvation,[3] and the cause of the calling of believers.[4] Christ's death specifically is the cause of the eschatological restoration,[5] and the *materia* of the believer's cleansing from sin.[6] Preaching, and the faith which attaches to it, are the instrumental cause(s) of salvation.[7] The frequency of such allusions shows that the idea was deeply imbedded in Calvin's view of salvation.

Now the question is in order: why did Calvin use this device? Surely he realized that the terminology was not biblical but philosophical and that in using it he was aligning himself to some extent with the scholastics, whose dependence on Aristotle he so often in other areas excoriated.[8] The answer can only be that in his judgment the usefulness of the device outweighed it liabilities. This illustrates that Calvin's opposition to scholasticism did not amount to a phobia, and that he was capable of making common cause with a distinctly scholastic idea when it was in his estimation true and useful. Nor did he feel compelled to condemn everything that the pagan philosophers had said, since he believed that by the common goodness of God these men, in spite of their unbelief, were often given keen insights into the natural order. Aristotle's observations on the various kinds of causation was clearly a case in point.

Theologically, Calvin used the fourfold causation scheme because it enabled him to express both the unity and the complexity of God's saving work for man. It was a systematic way of drawing together such diverse and temporally separate acts of God as election, redemption, and regeneration, placing them in

---

[1] CO 54:58.

[2] CO 47:156.

[3] CO 55:64, 55:109, 54:168.

[4] CO 55:224.

[5] CO 48:72.

[6] CO 49:395.

[7] CO 49:219, 49:438, 50:205.

[8] Cf. Aristotle, **Physics** 2.3.7, **Metaphysics** 1.3; Thomas Aquinas, **Summa Theologica** 1.19.8.

succession and viewing them as parts of one purpose. In such a construction, none of the causes is extraneous or dispensable; man's salvation is not more conceivable without calling than without election, for example. Election saves man, but election alone does not save man; redemption saves man, but redemption alone does not save man; calling saves man, but calling alone does not save man. The causation structure gave Calvin the liberty to emphasize whichever aspect of salvation he happened to be dealing with and to say that without it there is no salvation. This was not hyperbole for Calvin since each cause is necessary to effect the desired result. At the same time, Calvin never lost sight of the large divine plan of which the causes are an expression and which holds them in unity. Nor did he ever conceive of the series of causes in mechanistic fashion. The causes were simply the saving acts of the personal and sovereign God. The scheme was Aristotle's. The substance was Calvin's.

The balance which existed in Calvin's own use of this structure between the unity of salvation and the diversity of its causes has sometimes been missed by scholars. T. H. L. Parker, for example, saw a contradiction, an "ugly gap," between Calvin's doctrine of election and his doctrine of redemption through Christ. How, he asked in effect, can both be true? Either salvation is through election or it is through redemption.[1] Parker observed that Calvin sometimes spoke of salvation by election, and sometimes of salvation by Christ. But he interpreted this as a tension. Apparently he did not see that for Calvin both election and Christ were "causes" of the one salvation of God, and were therefore not to be seen in tension but in unity.

The same kind of mistake is possible when comparing Calvin's doctrine of faith with his doctrine of redemption through Christ. Calvin, as a Reformation theologian, would have nothing to do with *fides implicita*, or with a theology in which salvation comes in a wholly objectivized way. Man is saved through a faith which is personal, conscious, and willful. Only through such faith does the

---

[1] T. H. L. Parker, **The Oracles of God. An Introduction to the Preaching of John Calvin** (London: Lutterworth Press, 1947), p. 85.

work of Christ, as well as the election of God,[1] become beneficial. Christ cannot remain "outside of us" and still benefit us.[2] He must be received by faith for his death and resurrection to be of saving advantage;[3] the fruit and efficacy of his redemptive work come only through personal union with him.[4] Christ cannot be Redeemer at a distance.

Viewing Calvin's thought on this point through the theology of Amyraut can lead to serious misinterpretation. Amyraut believed that Christ's death did not become effectual except through faith; the effect of Christ death was latent, "suspended," waiting to be activated by faith.[5] Kendall, citing Calvin's statement that Christ's death remains "useless and of no value" until we believe, argued that this was Calvin's view too.[6]

The case is, however, that when Calvin made such strong statements on the necessity of personal faith, he was standing at the vantage point of the *causa instrumentala*, looking back, as it were, along the series of causes, and insisting that they do not cause salvation except through faith. But this does not imply that election and redemption were for him simply latent things which depend on faith for their efficacy. This is clearly not the case with election, for faith is not only the ratification of election but, seen from the opposite direction, the result of election. The same relationship holds true in the case of faith and redemption. The death of Christ is itself a cause, an act of God which carries within itself divine efficacy to accomplish the intended effect. So Calvin could also stand at the vantage point of the *causa materiala* and look forward toward faith as the necessary outworking of the

---

[1] Comm. on John 6:40, **CO** 47:147.

[2] **Inst.** 3.1.1.

[3] Sermon on Eph. 1:7-10, **CO** 51:288.

[4] Comm. on Gal. 2:20, **CO** 50:200; Comm. on Phil. 3:10, **CO** 52:50.

[5] For Amyraut, the efficacy of the death of Christ remains only theoretical or hypothetical until it is activated by faith. "Satisfactio Christi salutem integram nobis impetravit, . . . *sub eadem fidei conditione* . . . Filii donationem hactenus relinquit *in suspenso*, quasi nihil esset de ea determinatum." [italics mine] **Dissertationes theologicae sex** . . . (Saumur: Desbordes, 1660), pp. 290,156.

[6] Kendall, p. 16.

death of Christ. Viewed from this direction, faith depends on the death of Christ.

This is nowhere better illustrated than in Calvin's sermon on Judas and Peter (Matt. 26:67-27:10). At bottom, in terms of merit, Peter and Judas were absolutely equal: both fell into reprehensible apostasy by denying the Master on the night before his crucifixion. But from this point their destinies diverged. Peter was restored to Christ; Judas perished in his apostasy. Why the divergence? Calvin traced it to the passion and death of Christ itself. The point he made is not that Peter was elect and Judas was not (although this was assumed), nor was it that Peter believed and Judas did not, but rather that Peter was brought back from apostasy by the death and passion of Christ, and Judas was not. "The death and passion of the Son of God was to the salvation of the one, and pushed the other into condemnation."[1] The death of Christ *pushed* (*a poussé*) Judas to condemnation--strong words which suggest that in Calvin's mind the death of Christ was not only the effectuation of election, but also of reprobation. Christ's death did not, in this sermon, come to benefit Peter *because* he believed. To the contrary, Peter repented of his sin because God in mercy gave him a share in the death of Christ. The death of Christ was active power, creative grace, and *causa*:

> The death and passion of our Lord Jesus has already produced its effect and its power in that Peter has been raised from such a horrible fall . . . God displayed the infinite treasures of his goodness when he still made Peter sharer of the fruit of the death and passion of his Son.[2]

The death of Christ does not wait for faith. It generates it.

It is this conception of the death of Christ as an act of redemption which *effects* faith which must be overlooked in order to interpret Calvin as a universal redemptionist. A universal redemption cannot be a cause of salvation as Calvin meant it. For a universal redemption will necessarily remain ineffective for

---

[1] CO 46:874.
[2] CO 46:878.

those, namely the reprobate, for whom it was offered but who do not appropriate it by faith. Redemption as Calvin conceived it is not passive, suspended, or ineffective. It pushes through to its own effectuation, generates repentance and faith (as in Peter), and is in turn received by this same faith.

It is difficult to imagine that the fourfold causation scheme would have recommended itself to Calvin at all if he were a universal redemptionist. He set the *causa materiala* squarely in the line of divine causation that begins with election and ends with the eschatological blessedness of the elect. The very point of the scheme was that all the causes work toward the same effect. It would be contrary to the logic and the spirit of the whole idea if Christ's death, in lonely isolation, were universal in scope. Amyraut's theology is itself the best proof of this: in order to fit a universal redemption into a predestinarian soteriology, Amyraut had to posit two purposes and two directions of the divine purpose instead of one. He had, that is, to break out of the framework of a single line of causation, which necessitates limited redemption. In doing this he claimed to be breaking away from Beza's theology, but he was also breaking away from Calvin's.

The causation model recommended itself to Calvin because he had a unitary and systematic conception of the saving activity of God which was both monergistic and particularistic. Like election and calling, the death of Christ was for Calvin a cause of the salvation of the elect.

The Unity and Integrity of the Work of Christ

The topic of this section, Calvin's teaching about the specific parts of Christ's redemptive work, is one that is suggested to us by the work of R. T. Kendall. While Kendall claimed that Calvin was a universal redemptionist, he also recognized that Calvin taught that the priestly intercession of Christ was only for the elect.[1] Kendall's Calvin, that is, was a universal redemptionist and a "limited intercessionist": Christ died on the cross for every human being, then ascended to heaven to make intercession only for the elect. To use Amyraut's construction, it is as if Christ

---

[1] Kendall, p. 17.

suddenly switched from the execution of the *foedus hypotheticum* to that of the *foedus absolutum*.

This implies a bifurcation of Christ's saving work; it implies that part of Christ's work was for every human being and part only for the elect. Was this how Calvin saw it?

The redemptive work of Jesus Christ which Calvin called the *causa materiala* is, when viewed more closely, itself a complex of discrete but interrelated saving acts which includes his death, resurrection, heavenly intercession, kingship, and return. Calvin saw these works of Christ both in their particularity and in their overarching unity as the one redeeming deed of the Mediator. Here we must ask whether in Calvin's view the resurrection, intercession, rule and return of Christ--all the components of his work with the exception of his death, which we will come to later--were directed toward every human being or only toward the elect. As we find that Calvin directed these works exclusively to the elect, the claim of the Amyraut thesis, that Christ's death alone was intended to every human being, will look increasingly incongruous.

According to Calvin, Christ's resurrection was for the elect, its scope defined by the preexisting bond, established in election, between Christ as head and the predestined as his members. "For Christ did not rise for himself but for us. The head must not be separated from the members."[1] In a similar statement Calvin used the related term "church": "[the resurrection] was not only for himself, but for all his church."[2] Using yet another synonym for the elect, Calvin said that Christ, by his resurrection, entered into the kingdom of God in order to give to "his own (*suos*) eternal happiness."[3] The clearest enunciation of this doctrine of limited resurrection was the following comment on Acts 8:33, in which Calvin emphasized the unity of head and members and piled up the terms "church," "members," "his own," and "the faithful"--the vocabulary of election for Calvin--to denote those for whom Christ rose from the dead:

[1] Comm. on II Tim. 2:8, **CO** 52:363.
[2] Sermon on Isa. 53:7-8, **CO** 35:643.
[3] Comm. on Acts 13:34, **CO** 48:302.

This life [Christ's resurrection], which is without end, pertains to
the whole body of the church (*totum ecclesiae corpus*), since Christ
rose, not that he may live for himself, but for his own people
(*suos*). Therefore he extolls now in all the members (*in membris
omnibus*) the fruit and effect of that victory which he placed in
the head. Therefore every one of the faithful (*unusquisque
fidelium*) is able to form a sure hope from this place.[1]

The ultimate effect of Christ's resurrection is that his people share
in his resurrection on the last day. Calvin acknowledged the
doctrine of the general resurrection of both the saved and the lost:
all men must one day face the Judge in the body. He also
affirmed that the resurrection of the reprobate on the last day is
an act performed *by* Christ. But this is an altogether different kind
of resurrection from that of the elect, since it leads directly to
judgment. It is not a sharing in the risen glory of Christ, since it
is not rooted, as is the resurrection of the elect, in the
resurrection of Christ himself.

Now, though the whole world will rise again, and though Christ
will raise up the wicked to judgment, as well as believers to
salvation, yet as it was especially for the benefit of his church that
he rose again, so it was proper that he should bestow on none but
the saints the distinguished honor of rising along with him.[2]

In Calvin's thought Christ's resurrection leads to his ascension,
which marks his entry into the position of supreme power as king
and into the role of intercessor. As intercessor, he now faces the
Father in a priestly role and intervenes for the salvation of men;
as king, he faces the world and directs its events toward history's
predestined end. Both the priestly and the kingly roles have direct
and exclusive reference to the elect.

First, the priestly role. Calvin saw Christ's prayer in John 17

[1] Comm. on Acts 8:33, **CO** 48:194.

[2] Comm. on Matt. 27:52, **CO** 45:784. It is noteworthy that Calvin
could also speak of Christ's resurrection as the "life of the world" (cf.
Comm. on Acts 17:4) without meaning thereby all individuals.

as a prototype of his heavenly intercession, even though in time it preceded the crucifixion. Calvin noted that Christ prays "only for the elect," and "pleads with the Father in behalf of those only whom the Father himself willingly loves."[1] This was simply a repetition of the old Augustinian interpretation of this chapter. In a sermon on the ascension, Calvin stated that Christ took his place at the right hand of God in order to intercede for "his faithful ones" (*ses fideles*).[2] Calvin's conviction that the intercession of Christ is only for the elect even shaped his exegesis of Christ's prayer on the cross, "Father, forgive them, for they know not what they do." This prayer, reasoned Calvin, probably did not apply to all humans in a general way, nor even to all who were present at his crucifixion, but only to the ignorant multitude, whose part in the crime was unpremeditated.[3] Calvin balked at the idea that Christ prays for every human being.

Likewise, it is clear from what Calvin said that Christ's heavenly kingship is an exercise of his power and grace for the elect. It is true that such an office must involve the imposition of power on others than the elect; Christ is sovereign over the reprobate as well, and the world at large and even the devil come under the royal sway of the Mediator. For the present, their actions and even their thoughts are guided and controlled by Christ toward the accomplishment of his purpose. In the future, they will experience his kingship in the form of judgment. But this exercise of power over the reprobate is not the proper purpose of Christ's kingship. His is a redemptive kingship. Its central and soteriological meaning is something directed to the elect alone.

> So then, the kingdom of Christ extends, no doubt, to all men; but it brings salvation to none but the elect, who with voluntary obedience follow the voice of the shepherd; for the others are compelled by violence to obey him, until eventually he utterly bruises them with his iron scepter.[4]

---

[1] Comm. on John 17:9, **CO** 47:380.
[2] Sermon on Acts 1:9-11, **CO** 48:616.
[3] Comm. on Luke 23:34, **CO** 45:767-68.
[4] Comm. on John 17:2, **CO** 47:376.

As king, Christ saves, defends, and preserves his elect.

> Christ reigns to save his people, namely, when he brings his own
> (*suos*) to repentance and reconciles them to God.[1]

Christ as king is the "chief governor" (*summus moderator*), in
which office he accomplishes salvation for the church.[2] Through
the agency of the Son, the Father is the "eternal protector and
defender of the church."[3] For Calvin, the church on earth is an
embattled people, ringed with enemies, subject to the harsh
attacks of the devil, and utterly dependent on her Lord, in his
distinctly political office as king, for safety. Indeed, Calvin said
often that were it not for the kingship of Christ in the
preservation of the elect, the work of redemption and election
would be undone.

If Calvin conceived of the Mediator's work of resurrection,
intercession, and rule in such particularistic fashion, could it be
that he still saw the Mediator's death as universal? Was the death
of Christ capable of being thus isolated?

To answer this we must reckon with Calvin's concept of the
unity of the work of Christ. Even though Calvin recognized the
distinct aspects of Christ's work in his prophetic, priestly, and
kingly roles, these were not three separate offices for Calvin but
rather three parts of one office, that of Mediator.[4] The title
"Christ" (anointed one) pertains equally to the three roles.[5] So it
is quite clear that for Calvin Christ's work has a fundamental
wholeness and integrity which is reflected in the way Calvin spoke
about the relationship between Christ's death and resurrection.
The substance of our salvation is contained in the death and
resurrection of Christ, seen together,[6] so much so that to mention

---

[1] Comm. on Acts 5:31, **CO** 48:111.
[2] Comm. on Acts 7:36, **CO** 48:149.
[3] Inst. 2.15.3.
[4] Inst. 2.15.1.
[5] Inst. 2.15.2.
[6] Inst. 2.16.13.

one is always to imply the other:

> Whenever mention is made of his death alone, we are to understand at the same time what belongs to his resurrection. Also the same synecdoche applies to the resurrection: whenever it is mentioned separately from death, we are to understand it as including especially what has to do with his death.[1]

This would indicate that the scope of the death and resurrection of Christ should be the same. Is it possible in light of such a statement to maintain that in Calvin's theology Christ rose for the elect but died for every human?

Just as Christ's death and resurrection form a unity, so do his death and intercession. Calvin labored, in fact, to preclude the conception of Christ's intercession as an act divorced from his death. He did not envision a supplicating Christ, on his knees before the Father, but a sovereign Christ, stately and serene.

> For we must not suppose that he humbly supplicates the Father with bended knees and extended hands; but as he appears continually, as one who died and rose again, and as his death and resurrection stand in the place of eternal intercession, and have the efficacy of a powerful prayer . . . he is justly said to intercede for us.[2]

This was a remarkable interpretation. The very idea of Christ's intercession, Calvin was saying, is something of a metaphor. For this intercession is not really an "activity" of Christ at all, but simply the *presence* of the crucified and risen one at God's right hand in heaven. Christ's death and resurrection *are* the intercession.[3] Christ intercedes "by the sacrifice of his death," and his intercession is a "continual application of his death for our

---

[1] CO 55:269.

[2] Comm. on Rom. 8:34, CO 49:165.

[3] For Bucer, too, the intercession of Christ was nothing else but "the exhibition of the satisfaction of Christ" before the Father, who, seeing the blood of Christ, respects and receives it in our behalf. Cf. **Romans**, p. 413.

salvation."[1] The influence of his death functions as an eternal intercession for us.[2] "The blood by which he expiated our sins, the obedience which he rendered, is a continual intercession for us."[3]

Because Christ's intercession is the exertion of the power and efficacy of his death from his present exalted station in heaven,[4] the purpose of his death is brought to fruition in the salvation of the elect. Calvin insisted that the death of Christ cannot be ineffectual--it is "ever efficacious,"[5] nor will Christ ever allow the efficacy of his death to be destroyed or nullified.[6]

> [Since] he has given himself in such a way for our sins, he will not allow his death and passion to be unprofitable, nor the sacrifice which he has once offered to be void and ineffectual, without bringing forth fruit in us.[7]

> It is an unbearable blasphemy to think that the Son of God has descended to the world, has endured such a cruel death, that the judgment of God has thus fallen on his head, that he has borne the penalty of our sins, that he was reputed as the greatest evildoer of the world, and that nevertheless this should result in no profit to his faithful ones (*ses fideles*).[8]

This is, unmistakeably, the same emphasis which Gottschalk had made by saying that the blood of Christ cannot go to waste. The fruitfulness of Christ's death, implemented through his intercession, derives its certainty ultimately from election.

> It is also the object of Christ's prayer, that his death may produce, through the power of the heavenly Spirit, such fruit as had been

[1] Comm. on I John 2:1, **CO** 55:308-9.
[2] **Inst.** 3.20.20. Calvin also said, "Il a esté aussi declaré qu'il faloit que toute l'intercession fust fondee sur un sacrifice qui apres seroit offert." Sermon on I Tim. 2:5-6, **CO** 53:165.
[3] Comm. on John 16:26, **CO** 47:371.
[4] Comm. on John 16:28, **CO** 47:372.
[5] Comm. on Hebrews 9:25, **CO** 55:118.
[6] Comm. on Hebrews 10:12, **CO** 55:126.
[7] Sermon on Gal. 1:3-5, **CO** 50:294.
[8] Sermon on Isaiah 53:7-8, **CO** 35:643. Cf. also **Inst.** 4.1.2.

decreed by the eternal purpose of God.[1]

In this statement the predestination of God, the death of Christ, his intercession, and the agency of the Spirit are all brought together in a straight line pointing to the salvation of the elect. If the intercession of Christ is for the elect alone, and if it is really nothing other than the death of Christ itself, as embodied by the risen Christ in heaven, it would seem impossible to say, as Kendall did in defense of the Amyraut thesis, that in Calvin's thought Christ died for every human being but intercedes only for the elect.

While eschatology proper was not as fully developed in Calvin's theology as other soteriological themes, it was by no means absent. He viewed Christ's return as the necessary and culminating act of the Mediator, and as an act performed especially for the sake of the elect.

> Paul intimates that his resurrection would be in vain, unless he again appeared as their Redeemer, and extended to the whole body of the church the fruit and effect of that power which he manifested in himself.[2]

Though Christ's return, like his kingship, affects the reprobate, it is not for their salvation that he returns, but for the church. It is not an afterthought, but the essential consummation of the salvation of the elect, without which--and this we have come to expect in Calvin--all the preceding work would be in vain.

Calvin believed that the works of the Mediator, like the *causae salutis*, were both distinct and interdependent. They were directed to one end, the salvation of the elect. To recapitulate briefly what we have seen so far: Christ chose the elect, was sent by the Father to save the elect, rose from the dead for the elect, intercedes in heaven for the elect, rules for the sake of the elect in the present age, and will return for the elect at the end of the age. The Amyraut thesis calls upon us to believe that according to

---

[1] Comm. on John 17:1, **CO** 47:375.
[2] Comm. on I Thess. 1:10, **CO** 52:145. Cf. also **CO** 54:160.

Calvin, among all the works of the Redeemer, his death, in lonely isolation from everything else, was intended for everyone. It calls upon us to posit that in Calvin's theology the death of Christ did not fit into the larger purpose of which it was an integral, indeed central, part.

The Doctrine of Satisfaction and its Implications

Limited redemptionists tended to link the extent of redemption to the nature of redemption. Gottschalk saw the sacrifice of Christ in objective and unconditional terms and argued on that basis that those for whom Christ had died could never again come under God's curse. Bucer perceived, for the same reason, that the Anabaptist denial of *satisfactio* and their assertion of universal redemption were two parts of the same problem. And Reformed orthodoxy after Calvin grounded its defense of limited redemption, not only in the larger framework of predestinarianism, but also in the objective-legal interpretation of the meaning of Christ's death. Theodore Beza, engaging the believer in an imaginary conversation with Satan, put it this way:

> You say, Satan, that God is perfectly righteous and the avenger of all iniquity. I agree, but I will join to this another property of justice which you have left out, namely, that since God is righteous, he is content with one payment . . . God will not be paid double.[1]

What God has once and fully exacted at the cross, he will not, and cannot if he is righteous, exact again from the same person on judgment day. This concept of satisfied justice undergirded Beza's doctrine of limited redemption. Kendall noted the "no double payment" theme in Beza, and, characteristically, failed to appreciate that for Beza and other limited redemptionists this was preeminently a doctrine of assurance. Kendall also denied that the denial of double payment is to be found in Calvin. Is there any evidence of this concept in Calvin?

---

[1] T. Beza, **A Brief and Piththie summe of the christian faith** (London, 1565), pp. 21-21a.

Calvin viewed Christ's death on the cross as the substitutionary execution of divine justice. God punished Christ the Substitute for the sins of others. Because he stood judicially in the place of sinners, "he had to deal with God as an angry judge."[1] Thus the death of Christ was in one sense a transaction between the Father and the Son. But in another sense, because Christ was a substitute, it was also a transaction between God and the sinners whom Christ represented, for when Christ died something objective and forensic happened in God's relationship to those sinners. What Christ did in redemption was described by Calvin in several ways, all of them tied to the basic concept of substitutionary punishment. The most important of these are "payment," "appeasement," and "satisfaction."

Christ's death for Calvin was the payment of a price, not to the devil, as the early patristic theory had it, but to the righteous God himself. Man's sin makes him a debtor to God, but Christ steps in and pays the penalty of sin[2] and the price of redemption.[3] The image of payment speaks clearly of the objectivity of redemption. Other images make it clear, however, that this work of Christ is not some coldly commerical arrangement. There is personality and passion involved. For the God who demands and receives payment for sin is not a merchant but the wrathful judge and the creator, whose honor has been assaulted by sinful man. Calvin did not hesitate to speak of the "righteous vengeance of God" (*iusta dei ultio*).[4] Such fearful wrath is man's greatest danger, and must be turned away. So the effect of Christ's death, in relationship to this wrathful God, is to "appease" (*placere*) his anger.[5] This concept of appeasement was one of Calvin's most

---

[1] Comm. on Gal. 3:13, **CO** 50:210.
[2] **Inst.** 2.12.3.
[3] **Inst.** 2.12.5; **Inst.** 2.16.10.
[4] **Inst.** 2.16.5.
[5] Calvin said that Christ offered himself as a sacrifice "ut . . . placaret iustam patris iram." He came to gather us to life "by appeasing God (ut placato Deo)." **Inst.** 2.12.4. His sacrifice is to "appease the Father on our behalf (ad patrem nobis placandum)." **Inst.** 2.12.4. As a priest he appeases God's wrath ("placandum irae Dei"). **Inst.** 2.15.6.

characteristic ways of speaking about Christ's death. He even drew special attention to it in one remark:

> The word "appeasing" (*placatio*) is very important. For, in some ineffable way, God loved us and yet was angry toward us, until he became reconciled to us in Christ.[1]

The power of Christ's death to appease and thus to set aside the wrath of God arose in Calvin's thought from its objective-forensic character.

Calvin also spoke, most commonly, of Christ's death as "satisfaction." If God and men are to be reconciled, God's judgment must be satisfied. Christ fills this role. He offers his human nature as the "price of satisfaction";[2] he is, by virtue of his perfection, the only "adequate satisfaction," since all other men are polluted by sin;[3] by the expiation of his death he made satisfaction.[4] Often appeasement and satisfaction are mentioned in tandem as twin ideas.[5]

Calvin's use of the satisfaction theory raises the question whether his doctrine of redemption was that of Anselm.[6] While some slight variations have been detected--for example, that whereas Anselm viewed the sinless life of Christ as a meriting of life for himself, Calvin viewed it as part of the active obedience of Christ *pro nobis*--it seems clear that Calvin followed substantially in the Anselmian tradition. This was the conclusion of Doumergue, Emil Brunner, and Calvin's best recent interpreter, François Wendel, who stated, "We have good right to regard this last passage [**Inst.** 2.12.3] as a classic expression of the doctrine of

---

[1] **Inst.** 2.17.2.

[2] **Inst.** 2.12.3.

[3] **Inst.** 2.15.6.

[4] **Inst.** 2.16.2.

[5] Cf. **Inst.** 2.16.1; 2.16.10; 2.17.4; and 3.4.26.

[6] Anselm's theory of redemption (or of the atonement) is to be found clearly in his **Cur deus homo**, in **Anselm of Canterbury**, vol. 3, ed. and trans. Jasper Hopkins and Herbert Richardson (Toronto and New York: The Edwin Mellen Press, 1976).

satisfaction as it had been current ever since St. Anselm."[1]

One thing is indisputable: Calvin regarded the death of Christ as an objective-forensic event. The efficacy of redemption therefore does not operate through the moral influence it is able to exert upon human hearts as a great example of self-sacrificing love or heroism; its first thrust is God-ward, toward the judge, and only after this man-ward. Its efficacy comes through the settlement of God's righteous demands through payment, appeasement, and satisfaction. Calvin recognized the personal suffering of Christ, the struggle of his obedience in the face of such suffering, and especially the psychic agony of his profound separation from God. Once, in fearfully graphic words, he described crucifixion as a combination of the rack and the wheel. But never did he utilize the cross in a sentimental way, fixating on its gruesome details in order to stir up feelings of pity or remorse in his hearers. His theology of the cross was far distant from the medieval meditation on the crucifix or its later Protestant counterpart, the "bloody wounds" theology of pietism. The power of the cross for Calvin lay in its theological meaning, as the power of divine wrath appeased and satisfaction rendered. "His Crucifixion is a solemn, measured act of power--'the sleep of a lion'."[2]

The question must now be asked, did Calvin's doctrine of satisfaction lead him to a denial of "double payment"? The terminology of "double payment" does not explicitly appear, but in my judgment the substance of the idea does.

> We must, above all, remember this substitution, lest we tremble and remain anxious throughout life--as if God's righteous vengeance, which the Son of God has taken upon himself, still hung over us.[3]

---

[1] Wendel, **Calvin**, p. 219. Cf. also E. Doumergue, 4:231,233; Emil Brunner, **The Mediator** (Philadelphia: The Westminster Press, 1947), p. 458.

[2] P. Brown, p. 257. This is Brown's description of Augustine's view of the death of Christ; we have borrowed it here because it so aptly describes Calvin's as well.

[3] **Inst.** 2.16.5.

Because of Christ's death, God's vengeance is no longer a threat
to the believer; the comfort here lies in the theological meaning
of redemption itself as an act of appeasement. And again:

> But the main thing is that we know that the fruit of it [Christ's
> death] returns to us, since he tore up the writ that was against us,
> and acquired for us full satisfaction for our sins, so that we can
> appear before God his Father in such a way that even death no
> longer does us any evil or harm.[1]

Full satisfaction and the settling of God's legal case ("the writ")
against us assures that the fruit--by which Calvin meant the
application of Christ's death to the believer through regeneration
and faith--will certainly occur.

It is in Calvin's comment on Rom. 8:33-34 that the germ of
Beza's double payment idea appeared most clearly.

> The faithful are very far from being involved in the danger of
> condemnation, since Christ, by expiating their sins has anticipated
> the judgment of God, and by his intercession not only abolishes
> death, but also covers our sins in oblivion, so that they come not
> to an account . . . So there remains no condemnation, when
> satisfaction is given to the laws, and the penalty is already paid.[2]

Two phrases in this passage were significant. When Calvin said
that Christ's expiation has "anticipated the judgment of God," he
was saying that the death of Christ is the functional and legal
equivalent of the judgment which God will dispense on the last
day. In the act of redemption, a portion of final judgment has
been, as it were, thrust backward into history from the last day. As
such, the judgment meted out to Christ as the substitute is true
judgment--decisive, irrevocable, final. This is what led Calvin to
speak of the "satisfaction of the laws" having taken place in the
death of Christ, with the result that "the penalty is already paid."
And this is why, according to Calvin's exegesis of the passage in
Romans, Paul can triumphantly pose the rhetorical question: "Who

[1] Sermon on Matt. 27:45-54, **CO** 46:927.
[2] Comm. on Rom. 8:33-34, **CO** 49:164.

shall bring any charge against God's elect? It is God who justifies. Who is the one who condemns? It is Christ Jesus who died, yes, who rose . . . " The death of Christ, as an act of God's judgment, precludes any further exercise of judgment on those for whom it was made. This was Calvin's understanding of the passage. It is as close to Beza's double payment concept as it could be without using the very words.

In Calvin's comments on Rom. 8 the influence of Martin Bucer is again detectable. This is not surprising, since the passage was written in 1539, during Calvin's Strassburg period, and we know that he had read Bucer's own Romans commentary, which emphasized the doctrine of satisfaction in its interpretation of Romans 8.[1] Calvin did not, as Beza and later Reformed theologians, argue explicitly from the satisfaction concept to limited redemption. If there was an awareness of this connection in his mind, it remained unstated. But it is difficult to imagine that he could have espoused the satisfaction theory so vigorously, in the city where Bucer had defended it against the Anabaptists, and have held at the same time to the doctrine of universal redemption. As was suggested earlier, these things simply did not, in such a historical context, belong in the same cluster of ideas.

Theodore Beza may have developed the language of "double payment," but he did not develop the idea. It was present in the theology of predestinarians before him, Gottschalk, Bucer, and Calvin.

[1] Bucer, **Romans**, pp. 409, 412, 413.

8

CHRIST'S DEATH FOR THE ELECT

The only conclusion we can draw so far is that John Calvin *should* have been a limited redemptionist. His understanding of the relationship of the Father and the Son in salvation, his doctrine of Christ's relationship to election, his view of the redemptive work of Christ as one integrated thing performed for the elect-- from all of these vantage points we would expect him to teach that Christ died only for the elect. We have seen that in several crucial respects Calvin's theology was *not* what Amyraut claimed it to have been.

Still, the fact is that what Calvin *should* have been does not settle the matter. Perhaps he was inconsistent with himself. Perhaps, as proponents of the Amyraut thesis might claim, Calvin the biblical scholar was able to raise himself "above" his own predestinarianism and teach the doctrine of universal redemption anyway. So it is time for us to come to what Calvin said directly about the death of Christ.

What we find is that Calvin's language concerning the death of Christ pervasively reflected the consistent particularism of his soteriology.

To get the full impact of this, it is necessary to understand that Calvin spoke of the "elect" with a rich variety of terms, something that was probably a rhetorical necessity for a theologian who came back to the topic of the "elect" so often but whose literary sensibilities avoided repetition. When Calvin spoke of the "church" (*ecclesia*), "members of Christ" (*membra*), "his own people" (*suus*), "believers, faithful ones" (*fideles*), and "godly" (*pii*), he meant *the elect*. The elect or predestined, under all these designations, were for Calvin the objects of Christ's redemption on the cross.

Calvin frequently spoke of Christ as the one who redeemed

the *church* by his death. Not unexpectedly, this was closely linked
to the fact that Christ was also *author electionis*.

> And, certainly, it is not said that the church which he elected was
> found by him to be without spot and blemish, except that he
> cleansed it with his blood and made it pure and fair.[1]

Christ's office, given to him by the Father, was to gather for the
Father a church; indeed, *nothing else* has he been charged with.[2]
He is the "person to whom God has committed the charge and
office of redeeming the church."[3] Therefore, Calvin viewed Christ's
earthly life, in his public capacity as Mediator, as a work
performed in the name of (i.e. on behalf of) the whole church;[4]
moreover, Christ's representative labor for the church had as its
deepest theme and climax his death on the cross:

> We must always bear in mind the purpose of God in training his
> Son, from the commencement, under the discipline of the cross,
> because this was the way in which he was to redeem his church.
> He bore our infirmities, and was exposed to dangers and fears,
> that he might deliver his church from them by his divine power,
> and bestow upon it everlasting peace.[5]

So central was the cross in Calvin's concept of redemption that he
interpreted even this event in the early childhood of Jesus, the
flight of Joseph and Mary to Egypt to escape the anger of Herod,
in the light of it. He saw Christ's entire life as a preparation *sub
rudimentis crucis* for his giving of himself "to redeem his church."
So Christ was, characteristically for Calvin, the one who redeems

---

[1] Comm. on Luke 8:1-18, **CO** 45:356. Closely akin to this is Calvin's
statement that "Christ cleansed the church with his own blood." **CO** 45:367.

[2] Comm. on II Cor. 6:2, **CO** 50:75.

[3] Comm. on Matt. 12:18, **CO** 45:331.

[4] Comm. on Matt. 4:11, **CO** 45:130.

[5] Comm. on Matt. 2:19, **CO** 45:101-2.

the church,[1] who dies for the church,[2] the one who by his suffering and death exalts the church,[3] the deliverer of the church (*liberator ecclesiae*)[4] and the redeemer of the church (*redemptor ecclesiae*).[5]

Christ was also the one who came to save *his own people* through his death. God has established Christ as the "sole savior of all his people,"[6] and the one whose task it is to give life to all his people.[7] Christ accomplished this task preeminently through his substitutionary death:

> For the prophet expressly says concerning Christ, that he will deliver his own people (*suos*), not by pomp and splendor, but because he will endure the punishment due to their sins.[8]

> Lo, you see plainly that Christ bore the penalty of sins to deliver his own people (*suos*) from them.[9]

The terms *believers* and *faithful ones* were also synonymous with the elect in Calvin, because faith is the necessary outworking of God's election. Therefore, Calvin said, Christ's death was intended for believers. He died and rose to communicate life to all

---

[1] "In redeeming the church, says Isaiah, God put on his own righteousness as a breastplate." **Inst.** 3.11.12. "[Isaiah] teaches that Christ, to the end he may redeem the church, and restore her to life, must needs be broken." **CO** 48:193. "Now Moses takes for granted that the lamb was a figure of the true and only sacrifice, by which the church was to be redeemed." **CO** 47:422. "One peculiar consequence, indeed, which resulted from his death--that by it he redeemed his church--is altogether beyond the power of man to imitate." **CO** 51:222-3.

[2] Comm. on Eph. 5:25, **CO** 51:222.

[3] Sermon on Matt. 27:27-44, **CO** 46:905.

[4] **Inst.** 2.6.4.

[5] Comm. on John 7:27, **CO** 47:175; Comm. on Matt. 22:43, **CO** 45:618.

[6] **Inst.** 3.24.6.

[7] Comm. on Matt. 20:23, **CO** 45:555; Comm. on John 17:2, **CO** 47:376.

[8] Comm. on Matt. 27:38, **CO** 45:768.

[9] **Inst.** 3.4.30.

believers (*omnes fideles*),[1] and by the expiation of his blood he sanctified them.[2] In a phrase which clearly restricts the sacrifice of Christ's death to some and not others, Calvin spoke of "the believers, for whom this sacrifice was offered."[3] In commenting on Christ's final prayer on the cross ("Into thy hands I commit my spirit"), Calvin said:

> Let us now remember that it was not in reference to himself alone that Christ committed his soul to the Father, but that he included, as it were in one bundle all the souls of his own believers.[4]

A more vivid positive statement of limited redemption is hard to imagine. Here, at the very climactic moment of his sacrificial work, at the instant he delivers up his life to the Father, Christ according to Calvin brings with him *omnes suorum fidelium animas*, bound together in one bundle (*quasi uno fasciculo complexum esse*). That these souls are shortly afterward described, after the pattern of John 6:37, as "whatever was given to him by the Father" (*quidquid sibi traditum est a patre*), puts it beyond any doubt that this bundle of souls was, in Calvin's understanding, the bundle of the elect.

Calvin expressed the particularity of redemption with several other designations as well. Christ's death, for example, was the salvation of *the godly (pii)*,[5] and was for the gathering of the *redeemed (redemptos)*.[6] He bore the curse of the cross for "those whom he would call to salvation" (*ceux lesquels il devoit appeler à salut*).[7] And he took on himself the sins of *his members*.[8]

---

[1] Comm. on Matt. 27:52, **CO** 45:783.

[2] Comm. on Rom. 6:10, **CO** 49:109. Cf. also **Inst.** 2.11.4, where Calvin speaks of "the eternal sanctification of the elect" through the death of Christ.

[3] Sermon on Gal. 1:3-5, **CO** 50:299.

[4] Comm. on Matt. 27:50, **CO** 45:782.

[5] Comm. on Acts 13:30, **CO** 48:298.

[6] Comm. on II Peter 3:4, **CO** 55:473.

[7] Sermon on Gal. 3:13-14, **CO** 50:509.

[8] Comm. on Hebrews 10:5, **CO** 55:123.

There are passages also in which Calvin stated that the death of Christ was for *the elect*.

> Christ was sent as a Redeemer to the holy and elect people of God.[1]

> His death is called a perpetual sacrifice, by which the believers and elect of God are sanctified.[2]

In his commentary on the first chapter of Ephesians, Calvin utilized the fourfold causation scheme (which we have already encountered) to interpret Paul's exposition of the gospel. He found the *causa efficiens* in election and predestination, the *causa materiala* in the blood of Christ, the *causa formalis* in the preaching of the gospel, and the *causa finalis* in the praise of God's grace. He viewed the whole passage leading up to v. 11 as a systematic presentation of Paul's soteriology. Then he came to v. 11 and stated:

> Up to this point, he [Paul] has spoken generally of all the elect; he now begins to take notice of separate classes.[3]

This would certainly include the *causa materiala*, redemption through the blood of Christ, and would mean that the death of Christ--like predestination and faith in the same passage--is limited to the elect.

On another occasion, in a sermon on II Timothy 1:8-9, Calvin posed the question: "Who is it who has part and portion in such redemption as God has made in the person of his Son?"[4] Calvin knew that opponents of the doctrine of free election would answer this question in various ways, but all of their answers--those who choose God, those who seek God, those who submit to God,

---

[1] Comm. on Luke 1:68, **CO** 45:46.

[2] Sermon on Matt. 27:45-54, **CO** 46:924. This text also illustrates the equivalence of the terms "elect" and "believers" for Calvin.

[3] Comm. on Eph. 1:11, **CO** 51:151.

[4] Sermon on II Tim. 1:8-9, **CO** 54:52.

those who have good motives, those who are not coarse, those who are good-natured or devout (Calvin provided these sample answers)--would appeal to some quality or qualification in the person. Calvin called any such kind of answer "sacrilege." He explained to his hearers that the goodness of God can only be understood when we know that participation in the death of Christ depends on God's election. In other words, Calvin's answer to the original question was that only the elect have "part and portion" in the death of Christ.

For Calvin, then, Christ died for the church, for his people, for believers, for the godly, for those whom he intended to call, and for the elect.[1] Another designation for this same restricted group of people was the term *flock*, which Calvin derived from John 10 and used often in his commentary on John. The sheep of the flock are the elect.[2] And Christ is the good shepherd who dies for the sheep.

> From the extraordinary effection which he bears toward the sheep, he shows how truly he acts toward them as a shepherd; for he is so anxious about their salvation, that he does not even spare his own life.[3]

Christ is the great model pastor, who did not hesitate to shed his blood for the church (the term "church" slips in here quite naturally as a synonym for the "flock"),[4] and thus furnishes the example for all other faithful pastors in Christian history. Christ does not die because he is forced to die, "but offers himself

---

[1] When Calvin rejected the exegesis of Matt. 24:28 which states (in Calvin's words) that "the death of Christ had a sweet savor to draw the elect to God" (**CO** 45:665), he was not rejecting the doctrine of this exegesis but rather the suitability of the exegesis for this passage. On occasions Calvin had the ability, rare in the 16th century, to refuse to make doctrinal "hay" out of a passage when the hay was not there. At other times he was capable of throwing exegetical care to the wind for the sake of a polemical score.

[2] Comm. on John 10:16, **CO** 47:244; **CO** 47:145; **CO** 47:376.

[3] Comm. on John 10:11, **CO** 47:241.

[4] Comm. on John 10:12, **CO** 47:242.

willingly for the salvation of the flock."[1] It is only necessary to mentally substitute the term "elect" for the equivalent term "flock" in these statements to appreciate how consistently Calvin viewed the death of Christ in a limited way. It may be also that Calvin was influenced in this case by Augustine, whose comments on John 10 he carefully read.[2]

[1] Comm. on John 10:18, **CO** 47:246.

[2] **CCSL** 36:403 ff. Calvin showed his familiarity with this passage by quoting from it, though for another purpose, in **Inst.** 3.5.4.

9

CALVIN'S DENIAL OF
UNIVERSAL REDEMPTION

As pervasive and spontaneous as Calvin's references to Christ's death for the elect were, they do not yet, by themselves, constitute proof that he was a limited redemptionist. Theoretically, even a universal redemptionist like Amyraut could have said that Christ died for the elect, since in his view Christ died for every human, which certainly includes the elect. The acid test of a limited redemptionist is not whether he asserts Christ's death for the elect, but whether he denies Christ's death for the nonelect.

And Calvin did *deny* the death of Christ for the reprobate, clearly, and with feeling. We encounter this strand of his teaching, not in the **Institutes** but in controversial writings, and, most prominently, in Calvin's exposition of those New Testament passages which say that Christ died for "all" or for the "world."

Remark on the Lord's Supper to Heshusius

This passage is not an exegetical remark but a polemical thrust which comes in a rather testy pamphlet of Calvin's against a Lutheran theologian, Tilman Heshusius, who had entered the lists against what was, by 1561, already known as the "Calvinist" view of the Lord's Supper. This controversy foreshadowed the bitter strife between Lutherans and Reformed which would occur in the later sixteenth century. Calvin sensed the ominous nature of the exchange; he felt himself assaulted on all sides by Lutheran controversialists--Westphal, Staphylus, and now Heshusius--and cried out in rhetorical appeal to Melanchthon, now dead.[1] The days when a common Protestant front was conceivable had slipped

---

[1] **CO** 9:461.

away.

A lengthy discussion of the opposing eucharistic theologies is not necessary here. It is enough to say that the real point of difference between Calvin's doctrine of the Supper and that of Heshusius is whether unbelievers can be said to truly partake of Christ's body and blood. For Heshusius, Christ's flesh and blood are objectively present in the elements in such a way that even the blasphemous or unbelieving communicant eats and drinks them. Such eating, of course, is not salvific on the Lutheran view, but that is not the point for Heshusius; it is to affirm in the most incontrovertible way that Christ's body and blood are objectively present. Otherwise, he reasoned, we cannot really approach the Supper with faith. Calvin, on the other hand, said that Christ's flesh and blood are present in the Supper by the power of the Holy Spirit; the eating of Christ is not a physical devouring but a spiritual repast; and only believers truly partake of Christ in this way. He said, then, to press this point home:

> But the first thing to be explained is, how Christ is present with unbelievers, as being the spiritual food of souls, and, in short, the life and salvation of the world. And as he [Heshusius] adheres so doggedly to the words, I should like to know how the wicked can eat the flesh of Christ which was not crucified for them, or how they can drink the blood which was not shed to expiate their sins?[1]

Calvin continued by saying that this does not mean that Christ is utterly absent from the Supper even for the wicked. But he is present for them in the capacity of judge, not savior--"It is one thing to be eaten, another to be a judge." King Saul had the Spirit after a fashion, but was nevertheless reprobate, and likewise the wicked may experience Christ in the Supper but are devoid of the special communication of the grace and virtue which is received only by the elect. "Christ, considered as living bread and the victim immolated on the cross, cannot enter any human body which is

---

[1] CO 9:484-5.

devoid of his Spirit."[1]

This was a forthright denial that the body of Christ was crucified for the wicked and that the blood of Christ was shed for the wicked, in short, that Christ died for the wicked. Is it possible, in light of this statement, to save Calvin for the Amyraut thesis? M. Charles Bell tried to do so by using misdirection. He emphasized that Calvin consistently made the reception of Christ's body and blood a matter of faith and the Spirit. This, he maintained, was the touchstone of Calvin's doctrine in the remark to Heshusius; the passing reference to the apparent limitation of redemption is to be understood in light of it. So Bell explained:

> Calvin is *not* [his italics] discussing the atonement, but rather, the necessity of the presence of the Spirit and faith for the efficacy of the sacrament. He is definitely *not* [his italics] making a statement on the extent of the atonement.[2]

So Bell concluded that, because it can so easily be misconstrued (i.e. as a limitation of Christ's death), this statement should be regarded as "unfortunate hyperbole."

The problem with this interpretation is that Calvin *was* quite obviously discussing the extent of redemption. It is valid to point out, as Bell does, that Calvin in the same context emphasized the role of faith and the Spirit in the proper reception of the Supper. But there is no reason to suppose that this cancels out the force of what Calvin said about the extent of Christ's sacrifice. Bell is posing an "either-or": either the wicked do not eat Christ because they do not have faith and the Spirit, or they do not eat Christ because Christ did not die for them. But Calvin's theology combined rather than severed these things, and in the passage he was clearly saying that the wicked do not eat Christ *both* because they do not have the Spirit *and* because Christ did not die for them. The remark makes perfect sense in its plain and intended meaning.

---

[1] CO 9:485.

[2] M. Charles Bell, *Calvin and the Extent of the Atonement*, **Evangelical Quarterly** 55 (April 1983), p. 120.

Bell also said that if Calvin was in fact asserting limited redemption here, then he was contradicting what he has said earlier in the tract about the sacrament being offered to the wicked. Calvin did indeed say that the sacrament is offered to the wicked.[1] But there is no contradiction in this. Bell simply did not take account of the distinction in Calvin's theology between something being "offered" and something being truly given. Salvation is offered to the reprobate in the preaching of the gospel, and the body and blood of Christ are offered to the reprobate in the Supper. But salvation and the blessings of the Supper are given only to the elect. And Calvin's assertion that Christ was not sacrificed for the reprobate was simply part of his explanation of why they do not and cannot receive Christ in the Supper. Just as God offers the gospel to those whom he has not chosen, so he offers the body and blood of Christ to those for whom Christ did not die.

Calvin said: "I should like to know how the wicked can eat the flesh of Christ which was not crucified for them." No intelligent universal redemptionist would have said this, even in a hyperbolic flurry, far less a theologian like Calvin, who weighed every word.

Comment on John 12:32

"And I, if I am lifted up from the earth, will draw all men to myself" (John 12:32). We have seen the important role that this verse played in the discussions of redemption before Calvin. Universal redemptionists brought it up, and limited redemptionists always had to explain it.

Calvin dealt first with the words, "If I am lifted up." He said:

> Christ, being lifted up on the cross, shall gather all men to himself, in order that he may raise them from earth to heaven. The evangelist says, that Christ pointed out the manner of his death; and, therefore, the meaning undoubtedly is, that the cross will be, as it were a chariot, by which he shall raise all men, along with himself, to the Father.

[1] CO 9:483.

Calvin followed the gospel writer's intent, interpreted "lifting up" as a metaphor for Christ's crucifixion, and even affirmed twice--echoing the gospel's language--that this applies to "all men." Then he went on to interpret the phrase "I will draw all men to myself":

> The word "all," which he employs, must be understood to refer to the children of God, who belong to his flock. Yet I agree with Chrysostom, who says that Christ used the universal term "all" because the church was to be gathered equally from among Gentiles and Jews, according to that saying, "There shall be one shepherd, and one sheepfold" (John 10,16). The old Latin translation has "I will draw *all* things to me"; and Augustine maintains that we ought to read it in that manner; but the agreement of all the Greek manuscripts ought to have greater weight with us.[1]

Calvin had read Augustine on this verse. And, like Augustine, he interpreted "all" in a limiting way: it applied only to "the children of God who belong to his flock." The term flock, as we have seen, was for Calvin a synonym for the elect. So he was in effect limiting the scope of Christ's death to the elect. Obviously, the only conceivable motive for this kind of comment is to preclude the doctrine of universal redemption.

But Calvin's doctrine had another dimension. When he construed "all men" as the elect, he was considering Christ's death in its bearing on individuals. But he also recognized that the use of the universal term must have a positive purpose. If Jesus did not intend to teach that he would by his death draw every individual human being to himself, then why did he say "all"? Calvin found the answer to this in the interpretation suggested by Chrysostom, that "all" is a reference to Jews and Gentiles. This did not mean for Calvin that every Jew and every Gentile is included, as it undoubtedly did for Chrysostom, but there is still a universalistic intent to which Calvin sought to do justice. So his exegesis, like Augustine's, was designed to protect both the particularism of salvation and the universalism of the verse. This

---

[1] Comm. on John 12:32, CO 47:294.

dual concern will appear again and again.

Calvin's explanation of "all men" was obviously in line with Augustine's universalism of kinds; the substance of his exegesis was Augustinian. Yet, he mentioned Augustine only to take issue with his preference of texts,[1] and gave most of the credit for his view of "all men" to Chrysostom. This can only be because Chrysostom, and not Augustine, saw the real emphasis of "all" as the eradication of the barrier between Jew and Gentile. Augustine, strangely, mentioned many types of human groups and classes but said nothing about Jew and Gentile. Calvin was always aware that this great transition from the ethnic particularism of the Old Testament to the ethnic universalism of the New is taking place in the redemptive work of Christ. His exegesis of John 12:32 was therefore a skillful blending of Chrysostom's exegesis with Augustine's theology.

Sermon on II Timothy 1:9-10 (1555)

The text of II Timothy 1:9-10 says:

> [God] saved us and called us to holiness, not according to our works but according to his own purpose and grace, which he gave to us in Christ Jesus before eternal times, and has now manifested through the appearing of our Savior Christ Jesus, who has destroyed death and has brought life and immortality to light through the gospel.

This text furnished Calvin with a basis on which to expand, in a sermon of 1555, not only on the doctrine of election, but on the conjunction of election and the work of Christ. Paul, Calvin said, here joins together the grace of Jesus Christ with the eternal counsel of God.[2] This is to be seen both in the fact that election takes place, as Paul states, "before eternal times," and in the fact that election is revealed by the manifestation of Christ in history.

---

[1] Modern New Testament text criticism would agree with Calvin here against Augustine that *pantas* (all men) is the better reading. Cf. Nestle-Aland, **Novum Testamentum Graece**, 26th ed., (Stuttgart: Deutsche Bibelstiftung, 1979), p. 292.

[2] CO 54:54.

Because Christ is the revelation of God's election, he is the mirror in which we must contemplate our own election.[1] So several of the themes of Calvin's concept of the relationship of Christ and election, surveyed earlier, came to light in this sermon.

In this context, Calvin took time to emphasize to his listeners that the objects of God's saving work in this text are the faithful, and *only* the faithful. This meant, of course, the elect. He did this to meet a possible objection to his interpretation of the text.

> Besides, we note that St. Paul does not speak here of anyone but the faithful (*fideles*). For there are certain buffoons who, to blind the eyes of the ignorant and other like themselves, want to cavil here that the grace of salvation is given to us because God ordained that his Son should be the Redeemer of the human race, but that this is common to all, and indiscriminate.[2]

The objecters, whom Calvin raked with an *ad hominem* argument as "buffoons," would see in this passage a saving purpose of God which extends to every human being. Their reason for this, explained Calvin, is the belief that Christ came to be the Redeemer of every human being; if this is true, and if, as the Timothy text states, Christ's coming is the manifestation of God's eternal saving purpose, then God's purpose too must be for the salvation of every human being. So these "buffoons" deduce a universality of the saving will of God from the doctrine of the universal redeemerhood of Christ. This was no imagined line of reasoning: it had been made as early as the time of Augustine and as recently as the time of Bucer.

We must notice that Calvin went part way with the argument. He agreed that Christ is the "Redeemer of the human race"; this was one of his own favorite titles for the Mediator. It was not the language he objected to, but the content placed into it. For Calvin understood "human race" as the assembly of the elect from every kind of humanity. So he parted ways with the opposing point of view when it construed "Redeemer of the human race" to mean

---

[1] CO 54:54.
[2] CO 54:59.

"all in common and indiscriminately." The adversative *mais* marked this point of divergence in the sermon--"*but* that this is common to all in common and indiscriminately." Paul, said Calvin, is not saying that Christ is the Redeemer of every man without exception. Such an assertion is in fact a "cavil":

> But St. Paul spoke in another way, and his doctrine cannot be marred by such glosses and childish things. For it is plainly stated that God has saved us. Does this refer in general to all, and without exception? No, only the faithful are in view.[1]

Calvin limited the application of the whole text to the elect. God's eternal purpose in Christ is for the elect, and the manifestation of Christ in history is for the elect. The reprobate are not in view at all. Therefore, the cavil that Christ is the Redeemer of all men without exception is overturned. And to deny that Christ is the Redeemer of "all in common and indiscriminately" is surely tantamount to denying universal redemption.

This becomes even plainer if we consider how Calvin did *not* answer the objection which he himself proposed in the sermon. If he had been, as Amyraut thought, a universal redemptionist, he would have accepted the statement of the other side as a true one--that Christ is indeed the Redeemer of every man. But he would then have proceeded to explain that this fact does not militate against predestination, since Christ's redemptive work executes a different purpose from God's election, and that it is therefore improper to argue from universal redemption to universal election. He would have answered, in other words, that although redemption is universal, election is particular. He would have divided the question. This Calvin emphatically did not do. He accepted the assumption that election and redemption are linked as parts of one saving purpose, and limited the extent of both to the elect, the faithful.

Comment on Colossians 1:20

In his comment on Col. 1:20 Calvin faced the biblical

---

[1] CO 54:59.

statement that God through the death of Christ has reconciled "all things" to himself. Here the Greek is indisputably *panta*, all things, so there was no need for Calvin to discuss, as in the case of John 12:32, whether all things or all humans are intended. But the issue is in the end the same, since "all things" must surely include human beings. Therefore both Augustine and Bucer had felt compelled to explain the verse in a particularistic way.

The first question which Calvin handled in this text is, to what kinds of things *panta* refers, since it includes heavenly as well as earthly things. He concluded that it refers to rational beings, men and angels. After considering briefly how it is that angels are reconciled to God, since they did not experience a fall analogous to man's, he turned to another related question: does the universal term "all things" teach that Christ's work of reconciliation extends even to the demons?

> Should anyone, on the pretext of the universality of the expression, move a question in reference to devils, whether Christ is their peacemaker also, I answer: No, not even of the ungodly.[1]

Christ is not the peacemaker (*pacificator*) of demons, no, not even of ungodly men (*impiorum*). The term *pacificator* arises out of the immediate context of the Colossians text, which states that Christ made peace through the blood of his cross, and could only be in Calvin's mind a designation of the death of Christ. The term *impii* was one of Calvin's terms for the reprobate (just as *pii*, correspondingly, was a term for the elect). Calvin's answer to the question whether Christ died also for the demons was an argument *a fortiori*: if Christ did not die for the ungodly, then how much more impossible is it that he died for the demons? That Christ did not die for the reprobate was not argued here by Calvin. It was assumed.

Calvin was not by this saying that the demons and the reprobate are in exactly the same situation before God. He recognized that the "benefit of redemption is offered to the latter but not to the former." The gospel is preached to non-elect men

[1] CO 52:89.

but not to Satan and the demons. Still, this is tangential to the main point of the text:

> This, however, has nothing to do with Paul's words, which include nothing else than this, that it is through Christ alone that all creatures who have any conjunction with him cleave to him.[1]

This was an obvious echo of the exclusive universalistic exegesis of Augustine. Paul, said Calvin, does not intend to include every single rational creature within the scope of Christ's reconciliation. Rather, his intent is to *exclude* every other reconciler and savior except Christ. All creatures who are reconciled to God, whether men or angels, are reconciled through Christ and in no other way.

Calvin's exegesis followed closely the Augustinian pattern, reflected also in Bucer, of interpreting "all things" to mean elect human beings and the holy angels. But Calvin did not insist, as had Augustine, that the number of the elect must make up the number of fallen angels. He did, with Bucer, bring to the text a concern to deny that "all things" includes the demonic world. There can be no question that his exegesis was determined by the motivation which had also influenced Augustine and Bucer: to limit Christ's redemption to the elect.

Comment on John 11:51

In John 11:51 the Jewish high priest Caiaphas utters the following words: "Do you not realize that it is better for you that one man die for the people than that the whole nation perish?" Then comes the gospel writer's explanatory gloss:

> He did not say this on his own, but as high priest that year he prophesied that Jesus would die for the nation, and not only for that nation but also for the scattered children of God, to bring them together and make them one.

The text deals directly with the question, for whom Jesus would die; we recall that the Strassburg Anabaptists had adduced it in

---

[1] CO 52:89.

favor of universal redemption. Calvin's comment on it displayed certain themes that have already been noted and shows again that in his mind the death of Christ was only for the elect.

> Hence, also, we infer that the human race is scattered and estranged from God, until the children of God are assembled under Christ their Head. Thus, the communion of saints is a preparation for eternal life, because all whom Christ does not gather to the Father remain in death, as we shall see again under the seventeenth chapter. For the same reason Paul also teaches that Christ was sent, in order "that he might gather together all things which are in heaven and in earth" (Eph. 1,10). Therefore, that we may enjoy the salvation brought by Christ, discord must be removed, and we must be made one with God and with angels, and among ourselves. The cause and pledge of this unity was the death of Christ, by which he drew all things to himself; but we are daily gathered by the gospel into the fold of Christ.[1]

The point of Calvin's exposition was to capture the universalistic thrust of the gospel writer's words, which extend the effect of Jesus' coming beyond the Jews to the Gentiles. Calvin used the terms "human race" and "all things" to denote this: it is the human race which is scattered and in need of gathering; Christ was sent to gather all things; and Christ by his death drew all things to himself. Calvin identified this redemptive ingathering with the cosmic unification spoken of in Eph. 1:10--and, it should be noted, by extension, with that of Col. 1:20, a parallel passage. Christ's work is the removal of the "discord" which exists in a sinful world between God and man, and between man and man. Heaven and earth, Creator and rational creatures, nations and individuals have been set at odds by sin; Christ knits them back together by his death.

This begins almost to sound like Origen's vision of *apokatastasis*, the concept of the total restoration of all creation, and its implication, universal salvation. But it was not. Calvin was no universalist, and indicated even in this passage that there are some whom Christ does *not* gather into the fold. And this

---

[1] CO 47:275.

immediately compels the interpreter to recognize that when Calvin spoke of "the human race" and "all things" he did not mean every individual human being. The unification is achieved as the "children of God are assembled under Christ their head." In Calvin's mind the gathering of the elect from all humanity, and especially from Jew and Gentile, is effectively and representatively the reunification of the *human race itself*. That the reprobate are lost does not affect this assertion. The reprobate come almost to be regarded, from an eschatological if not from an ontological point of view, as non-creation. For God in Christ is nothing less than the Redeemer of the human race and of the world. Calvin would not weaken the force of this; neither would he allow that Christ is the gatherer, by his death, of every individual man.

The gathering of the elect, Calvin said, is a process spread out over time, which takes place as the gospel is proclaimed and believed. But it has a deeper source, which is the death of Christ itself, the "cause and pledge" (*causa et pignus*). The sense of this is, that because Christ gathered the elect to himself in death, they will be gathered in the process of history until the unification is complete.

In light of all that Calvin said here, his reminder that there are some whom Christ does not gather certainly rules out the possibility that he died for every individual person.[1]

Comments on I John 2:2

"And he is the propitiation for our sins, and not for ours only, but for those of the whole world" (I John 2:2). If there is any text in the New Testament which teaches universal redemption, this surely must be it. Augustine had interpreted "whole world" in this verse to mean the Catholic church as it is spread throughout the whole earth, the "mountain" which has filled the whole earth, the church which Christ has bought with his own blood.[2] It was clear in Augustine's comments on the verse that "whole world" did not mean every member of the human race, but rather the

---

[1] Augustine's treatment of this text was just as particularistic as Calvin's but said nothing about the death of Christ (**CCSL** 36:432-3).

[2] **MPL** 35:1984.

predestined. Still, what Augustine said about the verse did not so much emphasize the limitation of the death of Christ to the predestined as it did the universality of "whole world." Augustine used "whole world" offensively against those whom he perceived to be schismatics, whose great sin was to limit the church to a localized group and thus destroy its catholicity.

The situation was somewhat different for Bucer, and also for Calvin. For obvious reasons they did not use the verse exactly as Augustine had. In the sixteenth century the verse was being used against predestinarianism and limited redemption, and the need was to emphasize the limited scope of the phrase "whole world." Bucer had argued, against Hoffmann, that it must be understood of the elect. Calvin faced a similar challenge from a Sicilian monk named Georgius. This man, about whom very little is known, had the distinction of being the only opponent of Calvin's to directly attack the reformer's predestinarianism with one of the universal redemption texts of the New Testament. The significance of this will be discussed later.

Calvin's thoughts on this verse came in two explanations written closely together in time, in his commentary on I John (1551), and in **De aeterna praedestinatione** (1552). Having this stereo version of his exegesis is both helpful and complicating, for, although the content and aim of his remarks in both places were the same, the fact that in one place he was commenting and in the other polemicizing caused him to emphasize different aspects of his doctrine. First, his remarks in the commentary:

> Here a question may be raised, how have the sins of the whole world been expiated? I pass by the dotages of the fanatics, who under this pretense extend salvation to all the reprobate, and therefore to Satan himself. Such a monstrous thing deserves no refutation. They who seek to avoid this absurdity have said that Christ suffered sufficiently for the whole world, but efficiently only for the elect. This solution has commonly prevailed in the schools. Though I allow that what has been said is true, yet I deny that it is suitable to this passage; for the design of John was no other than to make this benefit common to the whole church. Then under the word "all," he does not include the reprobate, but designates those who should believe as well as those who were then scattered through various parts of the world. For then the

> grace of Christ is really made clear in a fitting way, when it is
> declared to be the only true salvation of the whole world.[1]

Here is a direct limited redemptionistic answer to the old
argument that the universality of "whole world" must include every
human being. Calvin also threw in, for good measure, the
argument that if "whole world" is absolutely universal it must
include the devil as well, familiar already from his exegesis of
Colossians 1:20. As in his comment on Colossians 1:20, Calvin
lumped the reprobate together with the devil and argued from the
assumption that what is true of one must be true of the other as
well. The doctrine that Christ's expiation is for the reprobate (and
by extension the devil) was to Calvin a "monstrous thing," one of
the *deliria phreneticorum*. It is very likely that Calvin had in mind
the Anabaptists here, since "fanatics" was one of his stock terms
for the radicals. If so, then his remarks here were a late
reverberation of the theological contests with the Strassburg
radicals.

Against the assertion of universal redemption, Calvin stated
that the expiation of Christ "does not include the reprobate," but
extends to "the whole church" and to "those who should believe."
Again we see the dual effort to limit Christ's death to the elect
while at the same time preserving a universalistic emphasis. There
was a clear echo of Augustine's exegesis, as well as of his concept
of exclusive universalism when Calvin summed up what he had
said by saying that Christ is the "only true salvation of the world."
His handling of the verse did not correspond at all to what we
should expect if he had been, as Amyraut and others have
claimed, a predestinarian universal redemptionist. He did not
accept the idea that Christ's death extends to the reprobate; he
did not accept the division of election and redemption into two
different decrees. His answer remained firmly in the Augustinian
limited redemptionist tradition.

We need to say something too about Calvin's interesting
comments on the sufficient-efficient scheme, but it will help first
to place in view his other rebuttal of Georgius, from the 1552

---

[1] CO 55:310.

treatise:

> [Georgius] thinks he argues very acutely when he says: Christ is the propitiation for the sins of the whole world, and hence those who wish to exclude the reprobate from participation with Christ must place them outside the world. For this, the common solution does not avail, that Christ suffered sufficiently for all, but efficaciously only for the elect. By this great absurdity, this monk has sought applause in his own fraternity, but it has no weight with me. Wherever the faithful are dispersed throughout the world, John extends to them the expiation wrought by Christ's death. But this does not alter the fact that the reprobate are mingled with the elect in the world. It is incontestable that Christ came for the expiation of the sins of the whole world. But the solution lies close at hand, that whoever believes in him should not perish but have eternal life (John 3:16). For the present question is not how great the power of Christ is or what efficacy it has in itself, but to whom he gives himself to be enjoyed. If possession lies in faith and faith emanates from the Spirit of adoption, it follows that he only is reckoned in the number of God's children who will be a partaker of Christ. The evangelist John sets forth the office of Christ as nothing else than by his death to gather the children of God into one (John 11:52).[1]

Again the question revolves around the meaning of "whole world." To Georgius this had to mean every individual. To Calvin, however, it did not. Rather, the teaching of the verse is that the expiation of Christ's death is extended to the "faithful" (*fideles*) as they are scattered throughout the whole world, and to the "children of God" (*Dei filios*), Calvin's language for the elect. The office of Christ is "nothing else than by his death to gather the children of God into one." This is a description of the doctrine of John 11:51, which, as has already been noted, Calvin would expound in the next year (1553) in a limited redemptionistic sense.

So the conclusion of this second passage was also that the reprobate are excluded from the "whole world." But the reply to Georgius penetrates a bit deeper into Calvin's theological thinking about the extent of redemption. The benefits of Christ's death

[1] CO 8:336.

come, in the end, only to those who believe (here Calvin adduced John 3:16), and therefore, because faith is the gift of the Spirit to the elect alone, only to the elect. This emphasis on the application of redemption to the elect through faith once more misled M. Charles Bell into an Amyraldian interpretation of Calvin's thought. According to Bell, Calvin rejected the doctrine of Georgius

> not in light of the extent of the atonement, but of faith. Because faith is the interpreting factor in this passage, Calvin can state that under the term "all" John "does not include the reprobate," but refers to all who would believe.[1]

Bell was saying that Calvin's restriction of this verse to the elect does not apply to the death of Christ itself but to its application. He was, in other words, viewing Calvin as the forerunner of Amyraut.

Once again, as in his analysis of Calvin's remark to Heshusius, Bell had something right and something wrong. He was correct that Calvin's argument here centered around the application of the benefits of Christ's death through faith to the individual elect. But he drew precisely the opposite conclusion from this fact from that which Calvin drew. Bell reasoned that because faith comes only to the elect, the expiation of Christ itself can still be universal in scope (although Calvin never said this). Calvin, in contrast, argued that because the benefits of Christ's death are in the end applied only to the elect, any speculation about the death of Christ which abstracts it from its actual effects is moot. The real point for Calvin was "not how great the power of Christ is or what efficacy it has in itself"--that is, how many people the death of Christ, considered in terms of its intrinsic virtue, could conceivably save--"but to whom he gives himself to be enjoyed." The real point for Calvin, in other words, was the *intention of God*. Augustinian soteriology always comes back to this in the end. If God intends to gather only the elect to himself through the death of Christ, then it is pointless to think of the death of Christ in any other way. Calvin affirmed that only those who will actually be *partakers*

---

[1] Bell, pp. 118-9.

of Christ (i.e. the elect) are the children of God; he said in the next sentence that the exclusive task of Christ is to gather these children of God, those who will one day be joined to Christ, to God *through his death.*

For Calvin, the limited scope of the application of redemption closed the scope of redemption itself. It is the divine intention which defines the extent of Christ's act of propitiation. And at this juncture Calvin's thinking was resting firmly on the more basic consideration that there are not two divine saving wills, one universal and one particular, but one divine saving will which is directed to the elect and only to the elect. The work of Jesus Christ, Calvin believed and insisted, derives its saving power not from some immanent mechanism--as if it would have somehow saved men even if God the Father had not wanted men saved-- but precisely because God ordains, accomplishes, and wills to accept it.

This focus on the will of God marks Calvin as a "strict constructionist" Augustinian. It also explains why he avoided the scholastic sufficient-efficient distinction as an adequate solution to the problem posed by I John 2:2 ("the common solution does not avail"). Calvin did not reject the device completely ("I allow that what has been said is true"), because there was, as we have seen, a way to construe this device in a limited redemptionist fashion. Wyclif had done so, and some of Calvin's own pupils and followers, men who were without any doubt limited redemptionists, would do so as well.[1] Why was Calvin dissatisfied with it in the exegesis of this text?

---

[1] Zacharias Ursinus, the chief author of the Heidelberg Catechism and one of those who are usually designated as "Reformed scholastics," spoke of the sufficiency of the death of Christ for every man in this sense: "It may be granted that the ransom of Christ is, because of its own worth, sufficient for the redemption of a thousand worlds. Nevertheless, it is properly offered only for those for whom Christ prayed, that is, for the elect alone." **Explicationum Catecheticarum D. Zachariae Ursini Silesii** (Neostadii Palatinorum: Matthei Harnisch, 1595), Part 2, p. 204. Kendall thought that the sufficient-efficient distinction had only the meaning given to it by limited redemptionists like Ursinus. He therefore drew the wrong conclusion from Calvin's avoidance of it in I John 2:2. Kendall, p. 16, footnote 2.

Because the formula, whether in its Thomistic or its "Wyclifian" form, does precisely what Calvin was arguing against as he rebutted Georgius: it provides a way of speaking and thinking about the sacrifice of Christ *as if it could be somehow detached from its divinely intended effect.* It was no part of Calvin's concern to find some theoretical way to posit that Christ died for every person, as Wyclif had done. Certainly Calvin believed that Christ's death could have redeemed a thousand worlds, not to mention every human being.[1] But this is entirely beside the point. He did not believe that that was the content of the term "whole world" in I John 2:2. For the extent of Christ's expiation is to be perceived from its effect, which is the expression of the divine will. Here, as always, the Augustinian axiom that what God wills must come to pass, and that what comes to pass is God's will, loomed in the background. And the effect of this expiation comes only to the elect. That settles it. So John's words, "the whole world," mean the "whole church," the "faithful," and the "children of God." Like Bucer, Calvin bypassed the subtleties of the scholastics and returned to the straightforward particularism of Augustine and Gottschalk.

Reply to Pighius

Albert Pighius[2], in his attack on Calvin's doctrine of predestination, had used the concept of the universality of

---

[1] Even at the high point of "Reformed scholasticism," the Reformed were ready to grant the sufficiency of Christ's death for all in this sense. The patently limited redemptionist Canons of Dort, for example, say that Christ's death was "of infinite value and worth, abundantly sufficient to expiate the sins of the entire world." **Acta Synodi . . . Dordrechti habitae** (Dort, 1620), 2:3. This did not mean for the authors of the Canons that Christ *did* so expiate the sins of every person. Amyraut's precursor, John Cameron, seemed to have recognized the double denotation of the word "sufficient." Armstrong, p. 59.

[2] Albert Pighius, a Dutch Catholic, published **De libero arbitrio et gratia divina** in 1542 both Calvin's and Bucer's predestinarianism. Pighius died suddenly in 1542, before Calvin's first response, **Defensio sanae et orthodoxae doctrina . . .** (1543) was published. In the 1552 **De aeterna predestinatione** Calvin again did polemical battle with the dead Pighius.

redemption (though no specific verses) to argue against predestination. When Calvin, in 1552, came to respond, he paraphrased the objection thus:

> That the gospel must preach Christ as the Redeemer of the whole world and of all indiscriminately appears to contradict particular election.[1]

This will be recognized as the argument of those whom Calvin called "buffoons" in his sermon on II Timothy 1:9-10, that the universal redeemerhood of Christ negates particular election. It is quite probable that in the sermon Calvin had this argument of Pighius in mind. His answer in the treatise was terse and completely clear:

> I respond briefly, that Christ is ordained for the salvation of the world in this manner, namely, that he saves those that are given to him by the Father; he is the life of those whose head he is; he receives those into the blessings of his fellowship whom God by the goodness of his grace has adopted to himself as heirs.[2]

This answer arose out of Calvin's Christology and out of his doctrine of the unity of the work of the Father and the Son and of the unity of Christ with the elect. Christ's redeemerhood extends to those given to him by the Father (the John 6:37 theme again), those whose head he is, and those adopted ("adoption" here, as often, was for Calvin a synonym for election) by the grace of God. Calvin, in short, defined the "salvation of the world" as the salvation of the elect. And salvation here, as the work of Christ, surely includes his death. A universal redemptionist in the mold of Amyraut would hardly have responded to Pighius this way; there would have been no need to do so.

---

[1] **De aeterna predestinatione, CO** 8:298.
[2] **CO** 8:298.

10

WHOM DOES GOD WILL TO SAVE?
CALVIN ON I TIMOTHY 2:4

"[God] wills that all men be saved and come to the knowledge of the truth." This text was always in the middle of any discussion of the extent of God's saving purpose. Origen had taken it as an affirmation of universal salvation. Augustine, seeking to uphold both the omnipotence of God and the reality of damnation, had argued that "all" did not mean *every*. Hoffmann had used the text against Bucer; Bucer had replied with the Augustinian universalism of kinds exegesis. And, predictably, Calvin's opponents hauled out the verse again, and Calvin, proving himself in this respect a completely loyal and unoriginal Augustinian, reproduced the exegesis of Augustine and Bucer. We get the impression, from the frequency of his remarks on it, that this was the text that always came up, that everyone knew about; you could not discuss soteriology in the sixteenth century without saying something about it! We may also assume that Calvin grew weary of plowing the same ground again and again and must admire all the more, for that reason, his persistence in so doing. This was the theological trench warfare of the sixteenth century.

Calvin's treatments of I Timothy 2:4

Calvin's earliest treatment of the verse revealed already the central idea of his exegesis, that "all" in I Tim. 2:4 refers to all *orders* of men, not to all individual men. This appeared in the 1539 edition of the **Institutes**, in the important new chapter on "Predestination and Providence." It is generally agreed that the theological influence of Bucer played a major role in both the appearance and the content of this section, and the fact that Calvin's interpretation of this pivotal verse followed Bucer's can only reinforce this assumption. Calvin said, responding to those who adduced the verse against predestination:

> The first statement of the apostle [i.e. I Tim. 2:4] is unsuitably adduced here. For it is easily seen from the context that the apostle there speaks, not of individual men, but of orders of men.[1]

Paul's purpose, Calvin explained, was to urge the early Christians to offer prayers even for the pagan Roman government officials. To counter any incipient notion that such people, declared enemies of Christ and persecutors of the church, are outside the reach of God's grace, Paul assures the believers that God wants all kinds of men, even the mighty, to be saved. "No order or condition of men is precluded from the way to salvation."[2] In the final version of the **Institutes** (1559), Calvin retained this original explanation of "all" but coupled with it another approach which he had incorporated along the way in the course of the intervening controversies. Noting that Paul says both that God wills all men to be saved *and* that they come to the knowledge of the truth, Calvin concluded that the second assertion qualifies the first: God's will, that is, is that all men come to salvation *through* the knowledge of the truth. Why then, Calvin asked, if this means every human being, has God not made the truth accessible to every human being? For it is clear from the biblical history that the knowledge of the truth was limited, by God's design and for long stretches of time, to the Hebrew people. "How did it happen that God deprived many peoples of the light of his gospel while others enjoyed it?"[3] Amyraut would argue that the limited extent of gospel preaching does *not* exclude anyone from the saving will of God.[4] But Calvin's conclusion revealed just how fundamentally different his theology was from Amyraut's (and how opportunistic or misinformed Amyraut's appeal for support to Calvin was): Paul, said Calvin, is not talking about all humans individually but about

[1] CO 1:888.
[2] CO 1:888.
[3] Inst. 3.24.16.
[4] **Brief Traitté** (1634), pp. 80-81.

the various divisions of humanity to whom the gospel comes in the new age. He also added, in 1559, this capsule summary:

> But since it clearly appears that he is there concerned with classes of men, not men as individuals, away with further discussion. Yet we ought at the same time to note that Paul is not stating what God does at all times, in all places, and to all men, but leaves him free to make even kings and magistrates sharers in the heavenly doctrine, though because of their blindness they should rage against it.[1]

Thus appeared in the final form of the **Institutes,** in a programmatic way, the important themes of Calvin's exegesis of this verse: God does not will every human being to be saved, but "all men" describes a universality of kinds.

Calvin alluded to I Tim. 2:4 while expounding I Corinthians 1:27 (in 1546) and Acts 17:11 (in 1560). In both cases the point under discussion was the extent of God's saving purpose. Although I Cor. 1:27 emphasizes that God's election favors the meek and lowly, Calvin added that this does not absolutely exclude the great, and offered I Tim. 2:4 as proof.[2] Commenting on the "nobles" of Berea who believed the gospel in Acts 17:11, Calvin cited it as a fulfillment of I Tim. 2:4, in which God extends his mercy even to the high-born of this world.[3] In both of these instances, Calvin was basing his use of I Tim. 2:4 on his understanding that it teaches a universality of kinds.

Calvin returned to the verse often in the decade of the 1550s, filled as it was with bitter battles over predestination. First there was the conflict with Jerome Bolsec in Geneva, which began in 1551 with Bolsec's public interruption of a sermon being preached by one of Calvin's fellow pastors, St. André, and which ended with Bolsec's expulsion from the city. In the legal process of Bolsec's trial, Calvin and the other pastors drew up a joint declaration on the doctrine of election in a display of solidarity against Bolsec.

---

[1] **Inst.** 3.24.16.
[2] **CO** 49:330.
[3] **CO** 48:400.

Calvin's opening statement was the longest of the individual statements, and in it he replied to Bolsec's use of I Tim. 2:4.

In this reply, Calvin followed the same pattern of argumentation which would later appear in the final edition of the **Institutes**. "If God wants all men to come to the knowledge of the truth, why has he sent no one to preach the gospel to the Turks?"[1] Why did the Spirit forbid the apostle Paul to preach in the region of Bithynia? It is apparent from this that Paul is not speaking of each individual human being, but of all estates or orders *(tous estats)*.[2] Lest the believers refuse to pray for those who appear to be only enemies of God, Paul urges this point. Calvin might be asked why, on his own principles, he was himself not more energetic in preaching to the Turks, but that is another matter.

The Bolsec affair prompted Calvin to produce a more complete exposition of his doctrine of predestination in 1552, the **De aeterna dei praedestinatione**. In this work Calvin used as foils both Albert Pighius (long since dead) and Georgius of Sicily. Both Pighius and Georgius had used I Tim. 2:4 against Calvin's doctrine of predestination.

Calvin answered Pighius first, in a passage which followed the (by now) familiar pattern: if God wants every man to be saved, why was his revelation given only to the Jews? Why did the Spirit forbid Paul to go into Bithynia? The real meaning of the verse, explained Calvin, is that Paul wants to urge prayer for the authorities, even those who are enemies of the church. Clearly, orders of men *(ordinum hominum)*, not individual men *(singulorum hominum)* are intended, not individuals within a kind, but kinds of individuals. Calvin's Latin--*non singulos generum, sed genera singulorum*--reproduces the wording that Thomas Aquinas had used to describe Augustine's universalism of kinds.[3]

Coming to Georgius of Sicily later in the treatise, Calvin simply pointed the reader back to the previous explanation. One brief comment shows his affinity with Augustine in an especially

---

[1] CO 8:112.
[2] CO 8:112.
[3] CO 8:303-4.

clear way, when he said that if the text means (as Georgius claimed) all individuals, then either "God is not master of his promises, or all men without exception must be saved."[1] This was simply Calvin's statement of the dilemma on whose horns Augustinians had always attempted to impale universal redemptionists and antipredestinarians: if "all" means *every*, then either God is less than omnipotent or every human being (and often the devil was thrown in here as well) will be saved. The doctrine of God's omnipotence, which had formed for Augustine the presupposition of soteriology, was also Calvin's foundation. Calvin did not hesitate to affirm Augustine's bold *dictum* that "the will of God is the necessity of things," and that future events therefore occur by necessity.[2] This thesis naturally leaves no room for God to will but not to attain what he wills. Hence Calvin's explanation.

In 1557-8 Calvin faced another challenge to his doctrine of predestination in the person of Sebastian Castellio, more famous as the author of one of the early arguments for toleration. His experience in Geneva no doubt had a great influence on him in this regard. Castellio used I Tim. 2:4 in his defense, and Calvin responded in the **De occulta dei providentia** (1558) and in a short tract in French which the editor of the **Calvini opera** traces to the year 1557.[3] In the former work Calvin repeated his standard treatment of the text in full,[4] and in the latter he limited himself to the question why, if God wills all men to be saved through the knowledge of the truth, he has not caused such knowledge to be extended to all.[5] These were, by 1558, time-worn themes in Calvin.

The question of whom God *wills* to be saved, raised by I Timothy 2:4, was obviously linked to the question for whom Christ died, since in everybody's theology the death of Christ was the expression of God's saving will. In fact, the biblical text of I

---

[1] CO 8:337.

[2] **Inst.** 3.23.8. Cf. also **Inst.** 1.18.3 for Calvin's espousal of the Augustinian doctrine of the divine will.

[3] CO 58: Notice Litteraire.

[4] CO 9:292.

[5] CO 58:201.

Timothy 2:4-6 itself moves from God's saving will to God's saving act in Christ when it continues by saying: "For there is one God, and one mediator between God and man, the man Christ Jesus, who gave himself a ransom for all" (vv. 5-6). Did Calvin carry his exegesis of "all" in v.4 on to the "all" of v.6, the "all" for whom Christ gave his life a ransom?

In two places, Calvin carried his treatment of the passage beyond v. 4 to v. 6. The first of these in order of time was Calvin's series of sermons on I Timothy, preached in 1554. The second was his commentary on I Timothy, dedicated to the Duke of Somerset (presumably one of those high magistrates to whom the grace of God had come!) in July of 1556. This indicates that for a period of approximately two years, from mid-1554 to mid-1556, Calvin was intensely involved with I Timothy.

Calvin's commentary on I Timothy 2:4-6

In the commentary, Calvin expounded v. 4 in the usual fashion. Paul is not speaking of individual men but is teaching that "no people or order is excluded from salvation." The text relates to "kinds of men, not to individual persons" (*hominum generibus, non singulis personis*).[1] This far his exposition was completely in line with his other treatments of the passage. Then, coming to the statement that Christ is a "ransom for all," he made it clear that the universe of discourse remains the same, for "this clause is of a similar import with the former." Then followed the application of the same universalism of kinds to the work of the Mediator which had obtained in the case of God's saving will.

> This Mediator was given, not only to one nation, or to a small number of persons of some particular rank, but to all; because the fruit of the sacrifice, by which he made expiation for sins, extends to all.[2]

Calvin was still employing the word "all" in the Augustinian sense defined in connection with v.4, but to preclude any possible

[1] CO 52:268.
[2] CO 52:269.

misunderstanding (almost as if anticipating the Amyraut thesis!), he added:

> The universal term [all] must always be referred to kinds of men, not to persons; as if he had said, that not only Jews, but Gentiles also, not only persons of humble rank, but princes also, were redeemed by the death of Christ.[1]

Calvin saw the whole passage as a unit. "The Holy Spirit commands us to pray for all, because our only Mediator admits all to come to him; just as by his death he reconciled all to the Father."[2] And he referred the universal term "all" throughout the passage to kinds of men, not individuals. Christ's death, like God's saving will, is directed not to every human being but to human beings from every segment of humanity. The whole case for Calvin as a limited redemptionist could well rest on this one place.

Two other things should be noted. The first is that Calvin's exposition, while carefully defining "all" in a manner compatible with predestination and limited redemption, still tended to stress the universalistic theme of the passage itself. Calvin the theologian believed that the word "all" does not mean *every*; Calvin the exegete knew that the intent of the word "all" is to include, not exclude. Unlike Gottschalk, he did not simply reduce "all" to "the elect" and leave it at that. He asserted repeatedly that God wants to save all, that Christ is the Mediator of all, and that this must serve for us as a warning against excluding anyone from the hope of salvation. We have already seen how Calvin used the passage to *include* the nobles and rulers. This hearty affirmation of what he considered to be a biblical universalism was one of the salient characteristics of Calvin's theology. It is also one of the reasons that scholars have mistakenly seen him as a universal redemptionist, not discerning the careful balance Calvin maintains between the universalism of Christ's death in its reference to groups and nations and the particularity of Christ's death in its reference to individuals.

---

[1] CO 52:270.
[2] CO 52:271.

The second observation is that Calvin did not handle the passage as he would if he had been, as Amyraut maintained, a proponent of universal redemption. This is becoming a monotonous observation, but it is nowhere more important to make it than here, in connection with I Timothy 2:4-6. We can well ask: what better raw material for the explication of the *foedus hypotheticum*, if indeed Calvin held this category in his theology, than this passage? For not only does the passage proclaim Christ as the ransom for all, but grounds this redemption in the saving will of God for all. One would argue from Amyraut's viewpoint that the passage is not speaking at all of the hidden will of God, which flows from election to the elect alone through the work of the Holy Spirit, but of the conditional will of God for the salvation of every individual. Amyraut himself, following Chrysostom and Thomas, said:

> And therefore these words, "God wills all men to be saved," necessarily receive this limitation, "provided they believe." If they do not believe, he does not will it. This will making the grace of salvation universal and common to all humans is conditional to the extent that without the accomplishment of the condition it is completely ineffectual.[1]

Had Calvin been the theologian that Laplanche, Armstrong, Kendall, and Bell thought him to be, he would certainly have done this.[2] But he did not. Instead, he drew God's saving will and Christ's death together under the absolute will of God and limited them both to the elect.[3]

---

[1] **Brief Traitté** (1634), pp. 89-90.

[2] Amyraut was in this specific point a better student of Calvin, for he noted that Calvin was one of those who interpreted I Tim. 2:4 in terms of a universality of kinds, not of individuals, though Amyraut attempted, for obvious reasons, to downplay the significance of this fact. **Defense de la doctrine de Calvin**, pp. 110-111.

[3] M. Charles Bell (*Calvin*, p. 119) claims that Calvin's limitation of "all" applies only to this single passage. This conflicts directly with Calvin's own stipulation that such universal language must "always" (*semper*) be interpreted this way; we shall see that Calvin followed his own advice.

Calvin's sermons on I Timothy

Beginning in September of 1554, and continuing through April of 1555, Calvin preached through I Timothy. In this sequence there was one sermon on 2:3-5 and two sermons on 2:5-6. This was, for Calvin, an unusual concentration of attention on just a few verses, and reveals the importance which he attached to the text. The same theology emerged from these sermons, though in a more practical and discursive style, as that which Calvin expressed in his commentary.

The general purpose of Calvin's sermons on this text was to emphasize what the text emphasizes: the universality of salvation. Paul tells us to pray for all, because God is the God of all, wants to save all, and has provided the Mediator's ransom for all. Calvin spoke freely to his congregation of the salvation of "all the world" (*toute le monde*). We are to pray for all the world;[1] God's mercy extends to all the world;[2] God declares himself to be the savior of all the world,[3] because the grace of Christ is extended to all the world.[4] Calvin also spoke in the sermons of "all men in general."[5] A casual look at such statements could easily lead one to conclude that Calvin was indeed teaching universal redemption.[6]

But such was not the case. For Calvin was extremely careful to explain, at numerous points in the sermon, that "all men" does not mean individual men, but groups and classes of men. This doctrine was for him not some refined subtlety reserved for professors and theologians, but solid food for the edification of the church. Even the common Christian is liable to be confronted by the antipredestinarian objection derived from this verse, that "God wills all men to be saved, that is to say, each person (*chacun*

---

[1] CO 53:147.
[2] CO 53:148.
[3] CO 53:151.
[4] CO 53:161.
[5] CO 53:149.
[6] Armstrong made just such a casual evaluation and as a consequence drew the wrong conclusion (p. 138, footnote 58).

personne)."[1] But Paul does not speak of each person but of "all peoples and orders *(de tous peuples et des estats)*."[2] This universality applies especially to the calling of both Jews and Gentiles to salvation.

As Calvin moved from the exposition of v.4 to that of v.6, he continued, as in the commentary, to think in terms of a universalism of kinds:

> But because St. Paul has declared that the grace which was purchased for us by the Son of God is common to all the world, that it is not only for Jews, but that it is also generally for all orders *(à tous estats)* . . . "[3]

Calvin's doctrine in both the commentary and the sermons on I Tim. 2:4-6 steered a careful course between two perceived errors. The first is that of the antipredestinarian, who attempts to argue from the universality of this passage against predestination; against this error Calvin argued that "all" means all kinds of people, not all individuals. The second error, and that which Calvin correctly perceived to have been the original concern of the text itself, is the limitation of the saving grace of God to some racial, political, or social segment of humanity; against this error Calvin proclaimed that Christ is the savior of "all the world" and of "all in general." This latter doctrine carries with it an imperative: Christians must desire, pray for, and work for the salvation of all peoples and all persons. There are no humanly perceptible *criteria* for distinguishing the elect from the reprobate. We must not shut off any man from salvation through our own prejudice.

Application of "universalism of kinds" beyond I Tim.2:4

Calvin was emphatic in the commentary on I Timothy that the universal term "all" must always *(semper)* be understood of classes and kinds, not individuals. Did he in fact do this himself? Was his exegesis of I Tim. 2:4-6, in other words, an emergency measure, or

---

[1] CO 53:151.
[2] CO 53:150.
[3] CO 53:175.

was it typical of a larger habit of interpretation?

The tendency to think in terms of universalism of kinds appeared very early in Calvin's theological writings, in his 1535 Preface to Olivetan's French New Testament:

> But when the fullness of time came, and the appointed time preordained by God arrived, this great Messiah, so promised and expected, came, and perfectly and completely accomplished all that was necessary for our redemption and salvation. And he was given, not only for Israelites, but for all men, of all races and regions.[1]

Here was the germ of the same conception which would be more fully used and expounded later. But we should not be surprised to find it expressed so early, for already by 1535 Calvin was an accomplished patristic scholar and had no doubt familiarized himself with the writings of Augustine. (Nor should we be surprised that Amyraut, predictably misinterpreting Calvin, cited this text to claim that Calvin believed in universal redemption!)[2]

Elsewhere, when Calvin encountered the universalistic statements of the Bible, he applied his own "*semper* rule" and handled them in ways which preclude all individuals. Regarding the words of Peter in Acts 2:17 ("I shall pour out my Spirit on all flesh"), Calvin said that the expression "all flesh" refers to men from all orders and ages, and from Jew and Gentile.[3] Peter's statement in Acts 10:28, that in God's sight no man is unclean, "is not to be understood of individuals . . . But Peter only compares Jews and Gentiles together in this place."[4] When Paul says that the grace of God has appeared, "bringing salvation to all men" (Titus 2:11), Calvin clarified, "Yet he does not mean individual men, but rather describes individual classes, or various kinds of life."[5]

---

[1] CO 9:801.
[2] **Defense de la doctrine de Calvin**, pp. 12, 24.
[3] CO 48:641.
[4] CO 48:239.
[5] CO 52:422.

In some passages Calvin used other techniques to interpret "all." When Paul in I Corinthians 15 says that at the return of Christ God will be "all in all," Calvin referred this to believers alone.[1] And when Jesus says, "They shall all be taught of God" (John 6:45), Calvin restricted the scope of "all" to the elect.[2] And, in a unique move, Calvin handled the assertion of I Tim. 4:10, that God is "the savior of all men," not as usual by restricting "all" to the elect, but by restricting the meaning of salvation to the general support and protection which God affords to all creatures, the "common benevolence" which we spoke of much earlier.[3] The end result is the same.

The Augustinian dike stood firm: In his exposition of salvation texts, Calvin never allowed *all* to mean *every*.

[1] CO 49:550.
[2] CO 47:149.
[3] CO 53:400.

11

CHRIST THE REDEEMER OF THE WORLD

Just as the proponents of the Amyraut thesis have often tended to minimize or even to ignore the body of evidence which has been presented up to this point, so have its antagonists often failed to do justice to the universalistic dimension of Calvin's thought on redemption. There was in Calvin's theology a powerful and pervasive depiction of Christ as the universal-cosmic savior, the savior of all men, *redemptor mundi*. Any real understanding of Calvin's theology at this point must rise above polemics, and above the desire to "claim" Calvin for some theological tradition.

What about the possibility that there were two "Calvins"--one who taught, in the stream of the strict Augustinian tradition, that Christ died only for the predestined, and another who taught that Christ died for every human being? The question must be posed and answered: was the Calvin who taught the death of Christ for the whole world still a limited redemptionist? A satisfying answer to this question must give to Calvin's universalistic utterances the full weight which he intended them to have. It will become clear that Calvin's presentation of Christ as the Redeemer of the world was not an occasional or accidental phenomenon, but one that lay as much at the heart of his Christology as his doctrine of Christ as the Redeemer of the predestined. So he must be allowed to say and mean what he intended. Better to end up with two contradictory Calvins who are real, than a plastic Calvin who is simply the product of the historian's logical finesse. At the same time, unless the evidence overwhelms it, there must at least be the presumption that he did not contradict himself on something as central as redemption. One can hardly read Calvin without realizing that here was a man who knew his own mind. Before settling for a schizophrenic Calvin, we must be convinced that when Calvin spoke, as he did in so many ways, of Christ as *redemptor mundi*, he intended to teach that Christ died for every individual human being. And a close look at the evidence will show that he did not.

The evidence to be considered here falls into four categories: Calvin's doctrine of the universal offer of the gospel; his exegesis of the word "many" as *all*; his direct statements that Christ died for all, for the world, or for the whole human race; and his statements about people perishing for whom Christ died.[1]

The universal offer of the gospel

Calvin clearly articulated a universal saving will of God that was conditional on faith, which consisted of the universal offer of the gospel through preaching. Amyraut, viewing Calvin through the prism of his own theology, mistakenly identified this with his own concept of the *foedus hypotheticum*.[2] But it was a quite different thing.

Calvin stressed that the gospel, and in it the benefits of Christ's passion and death, are offered to all men. In such contexts Calvin made it clear that "all" means all men individually. Calvin the Latinist provided Calvin the theologian with a variety of terms to articulate this doctrine: the gospel is offered (*offertur*) to all,[3] propounded (*proponitur*) to all,[4] set forth (*expositum esse*) to all,[5] and proclaimed (*publicando*) to all.[6] These terms all denoted for

---

[1] A great deal is sometimes made of the fact that Calvin refused to comment on the parts of the 6th Session of the Council of Trent which affirm that Christ died for all (cf. Basil Hall, p. 27; Kendall, pp. 14-15; J. Bray, pp. 111-112; Bell, *Calvin*, pp. 120-21). Calvin says, simply, "The third and fourth heads I do not touch (*non attingo*)." The statement is quite innocent of approval or disapproval and proves nothing.

[2] Armstrong says, "Amyraut shows that Calvin unequivocally affirmed a universal design for the atonement in his commentary on II Peter 3:9." Armstrong, p. 166. This is a glaring example of Amyraut's misinterpretation of Calvin. Calvin's comment on II Peter 3:9 affirms the universal offer of the gospel through preaching, not universal redemption.

[3] Comm. on Rom. 1:16, **CO** 49:19.

[4] **CO** 45:453.

[5] Comm. on Rom. 11:32, **CO** 49:229-30.

[6] Comm. on Eph. 3:10, **CO** 51:182.

Calvin the public preaching of the gospel through the agency of men. By this agency and means God invites (*invitare*) and calls (*vocare*) all men to salvation.[1] That "all" means all individual men Calvin indicated by the adverbs *indifferenter, promiscue,* and *sine exceptione* which almost always occurred in such statements.

Calvin usually coupled his affirmations of this universal gospel offer with the reminder that only the elect actually receive the gospel. For the public offer of the gospel comes always with the demand for faith, and only the elect have faith. So Calvin saw God here operating in two circles of human beings, one the larger circle of all to whom the gospel is publically offered through preaching, and the other the smaller circle of those who believe, the elect. This preached word is a kind of net cast into humanity at large which catches the elect and lets the reprobate slip back through. So there was in this sense in Calvin's theology a "twofold will" of God.[2]

This may look, at first glance, like the forerunner of Amyraut's two covenants, one wider and one narrower. But it was not. The crucial difference was that for Amyraut the death of Christ belonged to God's dealings with the wider circle of humanity, while for Calvin it did not. For Amyraut the gospel offer was backed up by the universal saving will of God and effectuated by the death of Christ for every human being.[3] For Calvin it was not. The universal offer of the gospel for Calvin was *only and simply* the public preaching of the gospel to all men; it was that will of God "which is manifested by the nature of the word, and is merely to invite by the outward voice of man."[4] If asked how such an

---

[1] CO 47:65; CO 48:36; CO 49:206; CO 45:75.

[2] Calvin's fullest discussions of what appears to be a twofold will of God were in his comments on Ezek. 18:23 (CO 40:446), II Peter 3:9 (CO 55:475-6), and Matt. 23:37 (CO 45:643-4). In none of these places did the death of Christ come into view in connection with the universal gospel offer.

[3] Armstrong said that for Amyraut "the work of the Son is the fulfillment of God's conditional will and the basis of the *foedus hypotheticum.*" Armstrong, p. 209.

[4] Comm. on Matt. 23:37, CO 45:643-4.

offer can be made to every individual when God's saving work and will do not extend to every individual, Calvin would not pretend to know. It is simply how God reveals himself.

For our purpose, the point must be that Calvin's doctrine of the universal offer did not, Amyraut's analysis notwithstanding, imply universal redemption. Armstrong's claim that Amyraut displayed a "sophisticated sensitivity to Calvin's theological position" was completely unwarranted;[1] Amyraut repeatedly pressed Calvin's thought into the foreign mold of his own theology.

The meaning of "many"

It was customary among limited redemptionists, both before and after Calvin, to point to several biblical passages where it is stated that Christ died for "many" as proof for the limitation of redemption to the elect. By this method "many" was understood in contrast to "all," as a limiting term, and the many were understood as the elect.

Calvin did not do this. Indeed, he asserted the opposite, that the force of the word "many" in such passages was not to limit but to universalize. This exegetical departure from the common method used by limited redemptionists confirmed R. T. Kendall in thinking that Calvin held universal redemption.[2]

Calvin's exegesis of "many" appeared in his comments on Romans 5:15 (1539), Hebrews 9:28, Matthew 20:28, Mark 14:14, and Isaiah 53:12. In all of these places the death of Christ is extended to "many." The comment on Romans 5:15 was the earliest of Calvin's treatments of this point, in which he first established his approach, and he sometimes referred back to it:

> But observe, that here a larger number (*plures*) is not contrasted with many (*multis*), for he is not dealing with the number of men.[3]

---

[1] Armstrong, p. xviii.
[2] Kendall, p. 13, footnote 3.
[3] Comm. on Rom. 5:15, **CO** 49:98.

Calvin rejected the approach in which "many" was contrasted with a larger number, not because he had a doctrine of universal redemption in the background, but because in his view the whole issue of numbers of men was not germane to the passage. So he took the exegesis onto altogether different ground. Paul, he said, is simply making the point that both Adam and Christ represent others, not just themselves. In regard to Heb. 9:28 he said:

> The apostle is not speaking of the few or of the many to whom the death of Christ may be available; but he simply means that he died for others and not for himself, and therefore he opposes many to one.[1]

Similarly, on Matt. 20:28, Calvin said that "the word many is not put definitely for a fixed number, but for more, for he contrasts himself with all others."[2] So "many" stands in contrast, not to *all*, but to *one*. Its effect is to broaden the scope of Christ's death from himself to others, and to make him a public and representative figure.

Calvin stressed that the others whom Christ represents are not just a few, not just "three or four,"[3] but "all," "the whole world," and "the whole human race."[4] We have seen how Calvin could freely employ such expressions without meaning every human being, and there is no reason for us not to read them here in the same way, especially in light of Calvin's insistence that the term "many" does not refer to numbers of men in any fixed or mathematical sense. For us whose vocabulary is so influenced by modern egalitarianism, it requires an immense empathetic effort to understood that a phrase like "the whole world" did not for Calvin mean every individual, but the effort is exactly what is essential to understand his theology.

There was some precedent for Calvin's method of exegesis of

---

[1] Comm. on Heb. 9:28, **CO** 55:120.

[2] **CO** 45:559. Calvin gave the same interpretation in his comment on Mark 14:24. **CO** 45:711.

[3] Sermon on Isaiah 53:12, **CO** 35:678.

[4] **CO** 37:267; 45:559; 45:711.

"many" even within the limited redemptionist tradition. Bucer had stated in his Romans commentary that the "many" of Rom. 5:15 meant *all* (though not *every*), but Bucer was also capable in other situations of taking it as a limiting term. It is surely no coincidence that Calvin's exegesis of Rom. 5:15 reflected Bucer's interpretation. Calvin, however, applied this interpretation consistently to the "many" passages whereas Bucer used it only once. Calvin was convinced on linguistic grounds that "many" was simply a Hebraism for "all," or for a large number as opposed to one. So his exegesis was not that of the preceding Augustinian tradition. But neither was it a repudiation of limited redemption.

Christ's death for "all" and the "world"

Calvin stated frequently that Christ died for "all," for the "world," for the "whole human race." More than anything else, it has been these kinds of texts that have led Calvin's interpreters to think that he believed in universal redemption. Despite his awareness of Calvin's interpretation of I Tim. 2:4, Amyraut took such terms of Calvin as descriptions of a universality of individuals. In Amyraut's published works such texts were cited in clusters, and phrases like *à tous*, *à tous hommes*, and *tout le monde* were italicized and thus accentuated. It worked amazingly well: Armstrong's Calvin citations showed a clear dependence on Amyraut's citations; Kendall's Calvin citations showed a clear dependence on Armstrong. Direct contact with Calvin, and with it the possibility of assessing correctly what *Calvin* meant by "all men" or "all the world," was thus lost, and Amyraut's (mis)interpretation taken as normative.[1]

An exhaustive accounting of such Calvin texts would fill many pages, so a short representative sample will have to suffice:

The world was reconciled to God through the death of Christ.[2]

The salvation provided by Christ is common to all mankind.[3]

---

[1] **Defense de la doctrine de Calvin**, pp. 12-14.
[2] Comm. on Titus 3:4, **CO** 52:428.
[3] **Inst.** 2.13.3.

He yielded himself to be crucified for the redemption of the whole world.[1]

Our Lord Jesus Christ appeared for the salvation of the world.[2]

This redemption was procured through the blood of Christ, for by the sacrifice of his death all the sins of the world have been expiated.[3]

The curse of all men was laid upon him.[4]

[Christ] has accomplished all things necessary for the redemption of the human race.[5]

The draught appointed for Christ was to suffer the death of the cross for the reconciliation of the world.[6]

The peculiar office of Christ was to appease the wrath of God by expiating for the sins of the world.[7]

This is only to scratch the surface. With his usual varied vocabulary, Calvin repeated this theme in every conceivable context. Christ was for him the universal savior, and his favorite designation for Christ, if sheer frequency of usage is any indication, was the exalted title *redemptor mundi*.[8]

But Calvin did not by "all," "world," or even "whole human race," used in soteriological statements, mean *every individual human being*. We have heard him clarify this point often enough; we have also heard him insist that this rule of interpretation should "always" (*semper*) be used--always, that is, in connection

---

[1] **Inst.** 4.17.5.

[2] Sermon on Gen. 25:28-33, **CO** 58:73.

[3] Comm. on Colossians 1:14, **CO** 52:84.

[4] Comm. on Gal. 3:13, **CO** 50:210.

[5] Sermon on II Tim. 1:9-10, **CO** 54:61.

[6] Comm. on John 18:11, **CO** 47:395.

[7] Comm. on John 14:16, **CO** 47:329.

[8] **CO** 46:844, 868, 895; 48:441; 49:95.

with the saving will of God or redemption through Christ. For in other connections, "all" clearly did mean every individual: when speaking of the universal sinfulness of the human race, Calvin meant absolutely every individual, and when speaking of the universal offer of the gospel he meant every individual.[1] The word was flexible for Calvin; theological context was everything. Sometimes the divergence of meaning crops up in one sentence: "As the human race was created in the first man, so it is renewed in Christ."[2] When Calvin spoke of the human race being created in Adam, he certainly meant every individual. But when he spoke of the human race renewed in Christ (which in the context is a reference to the glorification of the body at the resurrection), he could not have meant every individual. This illustrates the flexibility of the concept for Calvin, and his tendency to think, not so much in terms of numbers, as in terms of theological categories (i.e. Adam's people, Christ's people in this case). He viewed the elect as a kind of new humanity which was the theological, if not numerical, counterpart of Adam's children. In the same way, Calvin says that Christ came to restore what had been ruined in Adam,[3] and meant, not every individual, but the new creation of the elect. By the cross of Christ "the whole world has been renewed and everything restored to good order,"[4] which certainly did not mean that every human being will be renewed but that the fruit of Christ's blood is a new *cosmos*. And he said:

> Christ was appointed to be king over the whole world . . . that from every quarter would be collected the children of Abraham, so that the whole world would be the Israel of God.[5]

"Whole world" in this comment meant the children of God who, when gathered from every part of the world, form the Israel of God, the true church. It could not have meant all individuals or

---

[1] Inst. 2.1.4; Inst. 2.1.6; Inst. 2.6.1.
[2] Comm. on I Cor. 15:45, **CO** 49:558.
[3] Comm. on I Cor. 15:21, **CO** 49:546.
[4] Comm. on John 13:31, **CO** 47:317.
[5] Comm. on John 1:49, **CO** 47:36.

Calvin would be teaching universal salvation. In another passage
Calvin said "whole world" and obviously meant by it believers:

> The salvation of the whole world might be ruined, were it not that
> believers, supported by the hand of Christ, advance boldly to the
> day of resurrection.[1]

Here the "salvation of the whole world" was for Calvin the
perseverance and final glorification of believers; "whole world" did
not mean all human individuals. And when Calvin said that Christ,
at the Last Supper, thanked God "for the eternal salvation of the
human race,"[2] it is beyond any question that he was not equating
"human race" with every individual member of it.

So, Calvin typically said "all," "whole world," or "human race"
when he meant the elect. He assumed that his readers and hearers
would understand this; but not only did he assume it, he paused
in key situations to make it explicit.

Then why not speak simply of the elect, instead of "all" and
"world"? Was Calvin trying to be cryptic? Was he laying booby-
traps for people like Amyraut? No; to the contrary, there was
something positive to be maintained. Calvin's universalistic
language expressed the theological conviction that the elect,
chosen by God, redeemed by Christ, and gathered through the
Spirit from all places and peoples, constitute *a new and
representative humanity*. Calvin was not content to think of the
elect as a scrap of mankind or of Christ's redemptive work as a
desperate salvage operation. It was in fact the construction of a
glorious new world and a glorious perfected humanity. If there was
a scrap in all this it was for Calvin the reprobate. And this has
nothing to do with numbers; Calvin never speculated on the
numerical proportion of humanity which will be saved. This is not
known to man, and in any case it is not the point. The point is
that Calvin's use of "whole world" and other universalistic
expressions for the elect was a linguistic habit which flowed from
his theology.

[1] Comm. on John 6:39, **CO** 47:147.
[2] Comm. on Matt. 26:26, **CO** 45:705.

Underlying this was Calvin's extraordinary sensitivity to the great issue which permeates the New Testament itself: the extension of God's kingdom to the Gentiles. Calvin recognized that the great threat to early Christianity was not soteriological universalism (like that of a Pighius or a Bolsec) but ethnic particularism. The polemical battles of the sixteenth century over predestination did not blind him to the fact that the apostles--and especially in this connection Paul--were usually engaged in a very different kind of struggle. Christianity, emerging from the womb of Judaism, almost foundered on Jewish ethnic particularism. Even those Jews who became Christians still tended to see Jesus as a *Jewish* Messiah and the kingdom of Jesus as a *Jewish* kingdom. Paul fought tenaciously for a universal gospel, a gospel of Jew and Gentile, a gospel which in his view had burst the old containing wall of Judaism and had rushed out into the world. Calvin understood and felt this great transition. He exegeted Paul's letters from this perspective. The theme pervaded his commentaries on the gospels and Acts, and he saw everywhere in the Old Testament predictions and foreshadowings of it. Consequently, he viewed the New Testament universalistic language as testimony to the fact that God, in Christ, has redeemed both Jews and Gentiles and has made of them one flock.[1] The exclamation of John the Baptist, that Christ is the Lamb of God who takes away the sin of the world (John 1:29), Calvin interpreted in light of the extension of God's grace beyond the Jews to the "whole human race."[2] The lesson is the same with the title "savior of the world," which is ascribed to Jesus by the believing Samaritans in John 4:

> Christ testified that the salvation which he had brought was common to the whole world, that they [the Samaritans] might understand more fully that it belonged to them also.[3]

And the Ethiopian man who is baptized in Acts 8, realizing that

[1] Comm. on Eph. 2:16, **CO** 51:172.

[2] Comm. on John 1:29, **CO** 47:26.

[3] Comm. on John 4:42, **CO** 47:98. Cf. also **CO** 48:231 and 48:293.

the time of Jewish particularism is past, "confesses that Jesus is the Redeemer of the world."[1] Calvin, we might even say, was acutely aware that he himself, as well as the European Christianity of which he was a part, was *Gentile*; he knew that his own inclusion in the kingdom of God was the fruit of Christ's death for "all," and for the "world."

There were not two Calvins, but one, in whose theology were two distinct and complementary strands: one which viewed Christ as the Redeemer of elect individuals, and one which viewed him as the Redeemer of the world, that is, of all kinds of individuals. Amyraut mistook Calvin's universalism of kinds for the doctrine of universal redemption which he wanted to find in Calvin. That is the charitable way of saying it. A severer conclusion would be that Amyraut knew better, that he was aware of Calvin's qualification of "all" in the case of I Timothy 2:4, but went ahead and cited the texts for his own purposes anyway. Whatever the case, his interpretation of Calvin must stand discredited in light of what we have seen.

[1] Comm. on Acts 8:37, **CO** 48:197.

12

DO "SOULS PERISH FOR WHOM
CHRIST DIED"?

The best evidence on the side of the Amyraut thesis was
hardly tapped by Amyraut or his recent sympathizers: a numerous
group of statements to the effect that souls perish for whom
Christ died. The whole purpose of the doctrine of limited
redemption, as it flowed from the Augustinian premise of God's
omnipotence, was to make the number of those for whom Christ
died and the number of those who are actually saved identical. If
Calvin really believed that Christ died for some people who
eventually perish, then, it seems to me, we are back in a radical
way to "two Calvins."

Universal redemptionists had noticed the New Testament texts
that lend themselves to this interpretation long before Calvin.
Hincmar, we remember, had challenged Gottschalk with I Cor.
8:11 ("And so by this knowledge the weak man is destroyed, the
brother for whom Christ died."), and had argued, against
Gottschalk's insistence that the blood of Christ is never shed in
vain, that indeed it is. There is also Romans 14:15 ("Do not let
what you eat cause the ruin of one for whom Christ died."), to the
same effect. Gottschalk's treatment of the verse was weak and
tendentious. We expect something better from Calvin.

But Calvin did not perceive in this kind of biblical teaching a
threat to the doctrine of limited redemption. Elsewhere, he was
very sensitive to potential objections from the universal
redemptionist side, but when he dealt with these verses it was as
if they had absolutely nothing to do with the theological question
of the extent of redemption.

Apostasy and pastoral responsibility
Most of the Calvin texts in this category dealt with the danger

of apostasy from Christ and the church. The concept of blood-bought people perishing, suggested by I Cor. 8:11 and Romans 14:15, impressed itself deeply on Calvin's thinking about pastoral work and the mutual responsibility of Christians for one another in the church. It was an image to which he often appealed. We will cite these texts *in extenso* to provide the all-important element of context. And we will number them to facilitate our analysis.

#1. The apostle in the meantime exhorts us to be mutually solicitous for the salvation of one another; and he would also have us to regard the falls of the brethren as stimulants to prayer. And surely it is an iron hardness to be touched with no pity when we see souls redeemed by Christ's blood going to ruin . . . It therefore follows that we ought to regard them as brethren, since God retains them in the number of his children.[1]

#2. If the faith of one individual were in danger of being overturned (for we are speaking of the destruction of a single soul redeemed by the blood of Christ), the pastor should immediately gird himself for combat; how much less tolerable is it to see whole houses overturned?[2]

#3. Must we leave the poor church of God in the power of wolves and robbers? Must all the flock be scattered, the blood of our Lord Jesus Christ be trampled under foot, and souls which he redeemed at so costly a price go to destruction, and all order be set aside, and must we still be silent and shut our eyes?[3]

#4. And, indeed, just as God showed by an inestimable pledge, when he spared not his only begotten Son, how much care he has for his own church, so he will not allow the negligence of pastors to go unpunished through whom souls, which he has redeemed at so costly a price, perish or are exposed as prey.[4]

#5. So then, if the souls which our Lord Jesus Christ has bought so dearly are precious to us, or if we set so much store by God's

---

[1] Comm. on I John 5:16, **CO** 55:371.
[2] Comm. on Titus 1:11, **CO** 52:414.
[3] Sermon on Titus 1:10-13, **CO** 54:459.
[4] Comm. on II Tim. 4:1, **CO** 52:385.

honor as it deserves, it is certain that we will not bear with men's faults . . . To be brief, we must covet to have him be our brother, that God may be served by us all and maintained in his estate.[1]

#6. We ought also to have care for our brethren, and to be sorry to see them perish, for it is no small matter to have souls perish who were bought by the blood of Christ.[2]

#7. Will God then be held before our eyes as a laughingstock, all religion lacerated, poor souls perish who are redeemed by the blood of Christ, and abominations be gaped at?[3]

#8. When the weak conscience is wounded, the price of Christ's blood is wasted; for the most abject brother has been redeemed by the blood of Christ; it is then a heinous crime to destroy him by gratifying the stomach.[4]

#9. Even those that are ignorant or weak have been redeemed with the blood of Christ; for nothing would be more improper than this, that while Christ did not hesitate to die in order that the weak might not perish, we, on the other hand, regard as nothing the salvation of those who have been redeemed with so great a price. A memorable saying, by which we are taught how precious the salvation of our brethren ought to be in our opinion, and not merely that of all, but of each individual in particular, inasmuch as the blood of Christ was poured out for each individual . . . For if the soul of everyone that is weak is the price of Christ's blood, whoever for the sake of a little meat pushes back into death the brother who has been redeemed by Christ, shows his own contempt for the blood of Christ.[5]

#10. For to give up immediately on a man when he has sinned, or when he is, as it were, on the road to destruction, is to further the destruction of the poor soul that was redeemed by the blood of our Lord Jesus Christ.[6]

---

[1] Sermon on Gal. 6:1-2, **CO** 51:61,63.
[2] Sermon on II Tim. 2:19, **CO** 54:165.
[3] **De libero arbitrio, CO** 6:243.
[4] Comm. on Rom. 14:15, **CO** 49:265.
[5] Comm. on I Cor. 8:11-12, **CO** 49:435.
[6] Sermon on Deuteronomy 20:16-20, **CO** 27:631.

#11. Now I see a poor man going astray like a beast that is lost, and shall I allow God to be deprived of what is his or to have his possessions diminished? It is true that we cannot make him richer; but still, he shows how dearly he loves us in that he has purchased us with the blood of our Lord Jesus Christ. I see God's possession go to ruin, and I take no account of it, and so it is lost to him through my neglect--how shall I excuse myself? Therefore let us note well, that if we ought to maintain the welfare of mortal men because God has ordained that there should be faithfulness among us toward each other, we should endeavor and see to it even more that God may remain unimpeached in his estate, and that those who are of his house (that is, his church) may not miscarry, but that they may all be preserved for him.[1]

#12. "Which he purchased" [Acts 20:28]. This is the fourth reason with which Paul stimulates the pastors to do their duty diligently, that the Lord has given no small pledge of his love for the church by shedding his own blood for it. From this it is apparent how precious it is to him. And surely there is nothing which ought to urge pastors more vehemently to do their duty joyfully, than to consider that the price of the blood of Christ is committed to them. For it follows from this, that unless they faithfully carry out his work in the church, not only are the lost souls imputed to them, but they are also guilty of sacrilege, because they have profaned the holy blood of the Son of God, and have negated the redemption which he obtained, as much as in them lies (*quantum in se est*). And it is a most cruel offense, if through our neglect not only the death of Christ becomes vile but its fruit is also abolished and destroyed. And it is said that the church is purchased by God, that we may know that he wants it to remain wholly his, since it is right that he possess those he has redeemed.[2]

Did Calvin in these expositions slip out of his customary particularistic mode of thought? Did he really have in mind a theological doctrine of universal redemption?

The first step toward a proper understanding of what Calvin

[1] Sermon on Deut. 22:1-4, **CO** 28:9.
[2] Comm. on Acts 20:28, **CO** 48:469.

was teaching in these texts is to recognize that they dealt with the problem of apostasy. Those who profess to be Christians, and even seem by all outward evidences to be Christians, sometimes deny the faith or engage in some public and heinous sin which puts them outside the pale of the faith. This was a problem which was much on Calvin's mind, and was for him all the more acute because his ecclesiology. For Calvin was no mere advocate of the "territorial church." The church was for him the society of the saints, together with their children; its purpose was to manifest the holy life of the gospel as well as to preach the theological truth of the gospel to the world. There was for Calvin a genuine ethical dichotomy between the church and the world. He shared this, at least, with the Anabaptists he so detested.

Yet, in the hard reality of things, Calvin's church was the actual population of the city of Geneva. His continuation of the practice of infant baptism precluded for him the kind of sharp break from the past and clean start which the Anabaptists were able to make. His flock consisted of the same intractable human material which had been the population of Geneva before the coming of the Reformation, and only after time, the gradual exodus of the disaffected, and the influx of highly committed refugees from other lands, did Geneva begin to resemble that "most perfect school of Christ since the days of the apostles" which John Knox imagined it to be. And even in Geneva's heyday as the "Jerusalem" of Reformed Protestantism, the problems of sin and professed unbelief must have been items of daily discussion among the pastors.

So the problem of apostasy was a pastoral-practical problem, and the texts we have quoted indicate Calvin's approach to the problem: the pastor "must gird himself for combat." The doctrine of these texts belonged not so much to Calvin's soteriological teaching as it did to his doctrine of the visible church as it existed in history and geography, the empirical church which was seen by humans, and the church over which pastors were to exercise guidance and discipline. This is not to imply that Calvin could ever divorce ecclesiology and soteriology; these texts are themselves examples of how the truths of the gospel informed and shaped his pastoral practice.

There was, however, one all important consideration that influenced Calvin's approach to apostasy and discipline, which are the main topics of the "souls perish" texts: *pastors do their work in a state of imperfect knowledge concerning the souls of the members of the visible church.* I am convinced that this assumption, lying always in the background and sometimes in the foreground of Calvin's remarks, is crucial to an understanding of them.

The judgment of charity

According to Calvin, genuine and immediate assurance of salvation is the gift of God to the individual believer.[1] Through the conjoined work of word and Spirit, the believer is enabled to see in Christ the expiation for his sins and to know his own election. But this assurance is strictly private. The believer can know of his own election and salvation but he cannot know of someone else's. "The assurance of faith remains inwardly shut up and does not extend itself to others."[2] From this perspective Calvin's religion was extremely individualistic. But the radical individualism of assurance was not its only side. For Calvin recognized that the very existence of the church as an institution--in which he very much believed--depends upon some form of knowledge about the salvation of others. It is, after all, the society of the saints.

So Calvin posited, as the basis for the gathering of the saints together as church, a second kind of knowledge, which was qualitatively different from the individual believer's knowledge of his own salvation. It was a deductive and derivative knowledge which came through the observation of the evidences of salvation in the lives of others--confession of faith, participation in the sacraments, and the expression in life of the Christian virtues. When these things are evident, the conclusion is properly drawn that those who display such evidences are truly Christians. So, in

---

[1] Calvin emphatically rejected the medieval notion that assurance comes only through special revelation to some Christians. "Neque id ex speciali revelatione (quemadmodum sophistae quidam mentiuntur), sed ex communi piorum omnium sensu." Comm. on Rom. 8:33, **CO** 49:164.

[2] Comm. on Phil. 1:6, **CO** 52:9.

the place of absolute certainy, God has put

> a certain judgment of charity, by which we recognize as members
> of the church those who, by confession of faith, by example of life,
> and by partaking of the sacraments, profess the same God and
> Christ with us.[1]

Those who submit to Christ are, in the judgment of charity, to be
considered as his sheep.[2]

This judgment of charity was a frequent theme of Calvin's,[3]
and one which undergirded his concept of the visible church. The
judgment of charity was not a mere formality or rule of
convenience but a divine commandment which was to be zealously
practiced by Christians. Its purpose was to nourish love, concern,
and mutual regard, the very qualities which were at the heart of
Calvin's doctrine of church discipline. Calvin in one place even
explained the compassion of Jesus himself in terms of the
judgment of charity: Jesus' compassion for the Jewish multitudes
was not the soteriological love of God as such (which is limited
to the elect), but the attitude of a "public teacher," who for the
time was bound to regard all the Jews as belonging to God's flock
and church.[4] The judgment of charity, that the members of the
visible church are elect and redeemed people, provided even for
Jesus, as a public pastor, the assumption which was the basis for
his actions.

The judgment of charity had powerful implications. Most of
all it meant responsibility, for pastors but also for all Christians.
For if in the judgment of charity the church is God's flock, and
the members of the church God's elect, then to neglect one's
pastoral-brotherly duty to a fellow church member in spiritual
danger is to dishonor God himself. This is a point which Calvin
stressed in almost all of the passages quoted above. God will not
allow pastoral negligence to go unpunished (#4). God's honor is

---

[1] **Inst.** 4.1.8.
[2] Comm. on Phil. 4:3, **CO** 52:59.
[3] Cf. **CO** 49:312, and **CO** 55:207.
[4] Comm. on Matt. 14:14, **CO** 45:437.

at stake in the apostasy of a single church member (#5). Calvin even applied the Deuteronomic injunction about the restoration of lost property to its rightful owner to the problem of apostasy: to see apostasy occuring and do nothing about it is tantamount to stealing from God (#11). The heavy responsibility of pastors comes out most clearly in the comment on Acts 20:28 (#12). God has entrusted the immediate care of the church to pastors, and holds them responsible for its condition and the safety of its members from the depredation of "wolves." If the pastors fail, souls are lost and God is blasphemed.

It should be clear that Calvin was here regarding the church, not as a soteriologist but as a pastor trying to salvage apostates. The distinction that Calvin could make between Jesus as the omniscient Son of God and Jesus as a "public teacher" is the best evidence that there were two tracks in his thought. When he expounded the doctrine of salvation from a theological point of view his great goal was to establish the monergism of God and the infallibility of his saving purpose in the elect. But when Calvin exhorted pastors, he spoke from an immanent and empirical point of view, as if the salvation of souls were dependent on how pastors perform their task, and as if their failure would actually wreck the work of God. From this point of view it is possible indeed to speak of failure. Pastors must beware of losing what God wishes to be saved.[1] How different this is from the Augustinian doctrine that all that God wills must come to pass!

In other words, Calvin did not allow the doctrine of predestination to become the basis for pastoral practice, as if the fact of divine sovereignty in salvation could excuse sloth or lack of love. The basis for pastoral practice was to be the judgment of charity. The pastor could never say to himself, "I know that God will save his elect, and I know that those who fall away are not really his elect, so it does not matter how I perform my work." Predestination did come into the picture, but only when apostasy had run its full course in spite of the pastor's best efforts; then, it was a comfort to know that God had in fact lost nothing. But until this happens, Calvin vigorously called upon Christians to

---

[1] Comm. on Matt. 18:12, **CO** 45:505.

defend God's honor and estate by helping the wayward brother back into the fold of the church.

So the distinction must be made between Calvin's theological perspective of the church, grounded in election, and his pastoral perspective of the church, grounded in the judgment of charity, from which the pastor's marching orders come.

This distinction, however, was not an impermeable wall. Calvin was too much a predestinarian to ever let the sovereignty of God disappear from view; the omnipotence of God and the efficacy of redemption were much too important to completely ignore, *even* in this practical business of caring for the church. So the theological perspective sometimes found its way into Calvin's pastoral remarks. While stating that unfaithful pastors are charged with the souls they lose, and are guilty of sacrilege for profaning the blood of Christ, and have undone Christ's redemption--strong language which implies that the success of salvation depends on man, not God--Calvin added "as much as in them lies" (*quantum in se est*)(#12). This small phrase is actually a window through which the theological reality of monergistic salvation shines in upon the practical reality of human sin and failure. It was for Calvin a protective device, which he used often in similar contexts. Apostates, he said, are those who, "as much as is in them" (*imo quantum in se est*), crucify the Son of God again.[1] To despise a fellow Christian is, as much as possible (*qu'il est possible*) to deface the majesty of God.[2] Speaking of those who turn back to wickedness, Calvin said that "as far as they could (*imo quantum in se est*) they profaned and abrogated the inviolable covenant of God, which had been ratified by the blood of Christ."[3] Those who oppose the doctrine of election destroy, as far as they can (*entant qu'en eux est*), the salvation of the world.[4] And Judas, as much as he could (*quantum in se fuit*), would have ruined the purpose of Christ, which nevertheless stood firm.[5]

[1] Inst. 3.3.21.
[2] Sermon on Gal. 1:22-2:2, **CO** 50:358.
[3] Comm. on II Peter 2:20, **CO** 55:470.
[4] Sermon on II Tim. 1:8-9, **CO** 54:49.
[5] Comm. on Acts 1:15, **CO** 48:17.

The phrase was used too frequently and consistently to be without theological significance. It marked for Calvin the point where sinful human intentions come up against the immovable will of God and are frustrated. Men *intend* to crucify again the Son of God, to deface the majesty of God, to abrogate his covenant of salvation, to destroy the salvation of the world, and to ruin the work of Christ. But they cannot. Such things were theological impossibilities for Calvin. Still, this is what wicked men would do if they could, and the evil intentions of men, no matter how incapable of effectuation, are recognized as such and receive their due punishment from God. As always in Calvin's theology, man remained responsible and God sovereign. The phrase "as much as is in them," in its several variant forms, was designed to protect against the theological conclusion that the wicked acts of men can ever actually harm or thwart the design of God.

The point at issue--whether Calvin's "souls perish" statements imply universal redemption--may now be directly addressed. For Calvin used this phrase also in conjunction with the nullification of the death of Christ that seemingly happens when someone apostatizes. He said that unfaithful pastors "have negated the redemption which he obtained." But does this actually mean that pastors can undo the work of Christ by their sloth? No, for Calvin added, *"quantum in se est"* (#12), meaning that, although negligent pastors act as if they intend to negate Christ's redemption, they cannot. They come under severe judgment for their sin, but their intentions come to nought. Calvin also spoke of the death of Christ in the passage alluded to above (comment on II Peter 2:20): those who apostatize from Christ profane and abrogate the covenant of God ratified by the blood of Christ *imo quantum in se est*. Again, the idea is not that God's covenant in Christ's blood can be frustrated, but that wicked men *intend* to do so by their actions and attitudes. In a comment on Jude v.4 Calvin says:

> He means that "Christ is denied" when they who had been redeemed by his blood become again the vassals of the devil, and thus make void, as far as they can (*quantum in se est*), that

incomparable price.[1]

As an Augustinian theologian, Calvin did not believe that the "incomparable price" of Christ's blood could be made void, as it would indeed be if those whom he redeemed turned back to the devil. That is why he qualified and protected this whole statement with *quantum in se est.* Yet, inasmuch as these apostates have been incorporated into the church, have professed to be redeemed by Christ, have participated in the sacraments of redemption, and have publicly borne the name of Christ, their renunciation of redemption is a terribly serious matter. They are, from the point of view of their intention, and from the point of view of the judgment of charity and pastoral practice, destroying the work of Christ.

Calvin's many statements about souls perishing for whom Christ died must be understood in this context of practical pastoral theology and his view of the visible church. From the point of view of the judgment of charity and pastoral responsibility, souls perish for whom Christ died; from the point of view of God's omnipotence, predestination, and Christ's redemption, souls cannot perish for whom Christ died. And if proponents of the Amyraut thesis should insist that these texts prove universal redemption, then not only do they prove that some perish for whom Christ died--they prove (to replicate Calvin's language) that Christ's death can be negated, ruined, and destroyed by man, that the honor and possession of God can be stolen from him by man, and so on. And this is too much for Calvin's theology to bear. The case is, that because of his theology of the visible church and his belief in the judgment of charity, he spoke of the church member as a soul bought by the blood of Christ, whose apostasy is to be *regarded* as nothing less than the loss of Christ's rightful possession, the overturning of God's covenant, and the thwarting of his will. On this basis pastors and all Christians must exert every effort to combat apostasy. They cannot take refuge from this responsibility in predestination. The church must proceed *as if* every member is elect, *as if* every

---

[1] Comm. on Jude 4, **CO** 55:490.

member is redeemed by the blood of Christ, and *as if* the loss of souls from the visible church is therefore loss to the honor of God.

So understood, the "souls perish" passages do not militate against Calvin's teaching elsewhere that Christ's death is limited to the elect. In fact, on close inspection, we observe that in these texts Calvin said nothing whatever about Christ dying for every human. Instead, it is the visible church which is the circle of humans purchased by the blood of Christ, and by the judgment of charity the soul who is in the visible church is to be regarded as the redeemed possession of Christ. The blood of Christ is the manifestation of God's care for "his own church" (#4); "the Lord has given no small pledge of his love for the church by shedding his own blood for it" (#12); "and it is said that the church is purchased by God, that we may know that he wants it to remain wholly his, since it is right that he possess those he has redeemed" (#12). The doctrine of limited redemption (*Christus redemptor ecclesiae*) coverged here with the judgment of charity. Yet it would be ludicrous to conclude from this that Calvin believed, from a strictly theological point of view, that Christ died for all who are in the visible church. The two vantage points must be distinguished.

Souls perishing outside the church

There is another, smaller group of "souls perish" passages which deal, not with the visible church, but with unbelieving men at large. This group of texts poses a somewhat different issue from those discussed already.

> However, St. Paul speaks here expressly of the saints or faithful, but this does not imply that we should not pray generally for all men. For the wretched unbelievers and the ignorant have great need to be pleaded for with God; behold them on the way to destruction. If we saw a beast at the point of perishing, we would have pity on it. And what shall we do when we see souls in peril, which are so precious before God, as he has shown in that he has redeemed them with the blood of his own Son? If we see then a poor soul going to destruction, ought we not to be moved with compassion and kindness, and should we not desire God to apply the remedy? So then, Paul's meaning in this passage is not that

we should let the wretched unbelievers alone without having any care for them. We should pray generally for all men.[1]

The teaching here has certain features in common with Calvin's teaching on apostasy. His purpose was to motivate his hearers to redemptive action toward those who need help. And he used the death of Christ for others to establish the value of their souls and their worthiness of our concern. The main difference is that here Calvin was not speaking of those within the church, but of "wretched unbelievers" outside it, people who are manifestly not Christians.

Did Calvin mean that Christ died for every one of these wretched unbelievers? Did Calvin base his exhortation to pray for all men on the doctrine that Christ died for all individuals? Before this question can be answered, we must take some account of Calvin's general view of the activities of Christians toward unbelievers. The most important of these activities are prayer and preaching. As in the case of church discipline and pastoral care, Calvin believed that Christian activity must be based, not on the elective decree of God (about which we have no firm knowledge in cases other than our own), but on a practical working assumption. The assumption in the case of unbelievers was one which dovetailed with the universal saving will of God revealed in preaching: God loves all sinners and wills all sinners to be saved. This, as we have seen, was not for Calvin theologically true. But it was the assumption which has to be made concerning Christian activity toward the world of men outside the church.

Calvin explained this assumption several times. He cautioned, for example, against desiring vengeance against any specific person, since we have been told to desire the good of all men.

Although we may in a general way desire vengeance against the reprobate, yet, because we cannot as yet distinguish them, we ought to desire the welfare of all.[2]

---

[1] Sermon on Eph. 6:18-19, **CO** 51:842.
[2] Comm. on II Thess. 1:8, **CO** 52:191.

The preaching of the gospel must also be governed by the same principle:

> Since the ministers of the gospel, and those who are called to the office of teaching, cannot distinguish between the children of God and the swine, it is their duty to present the doctrine of salvation indiscriminately to all.[1]

> Faithful teachers ought to endeavor to gather all to Christ; and since they cannot distinguish between sheep and wild beasts, they ought to try by all methods if possible to tame those who resemble wolves rather than sheep.[2]

Moreover, the prayers that God commands for all men are also based on ignorance of the precise identity of the elect and reprobate. Even Christ, in his office as public teacher, prayed indiscriminately for all (although in his office as redeemer and Mediator he prays only for the elect). Therefore we must pray for each individual man *as if* he were one of God's elect, since in our present state of partial perception we cannot discern anyone's election but our own. Still, Calvin pointed out, from God's point of view such prayers are heard and answered only for the elect.[3]

This brings us back to the original quotation, in which Calvin used the death of Christ for "wretched unbelievers" as motivation to pray for them. Did this express, not a dogmatic truth, but a working assumption based on ignorance? The following parallel passage would seem to justify an affirmative answer to this question:

> What should we do but pray to God for those who are on the way to destruction? Indeed, has not our Lord Jesus Christ redeemed men's souls? It is true that the effect [of his death] does not come to all the world; but still, because it is not ours to distinguish between the righteous and sinners who are going to destruction, Jesus Christ has endured death and suffering for them

---

[1] Comm. on Matt. 7:6, **CO** 45:216.
[2] Comm. on John 21:16, **CO** 47:453.
[3] Comm. on John 17:9, **CO** 47:380.

as well as for us.[1]

The themes of prayer for all, efforts on the part of Christians to save all, and the death of Christ for all were woven together in this passage. What comes through with clarity is that the death of Christ for all--"for them as well as for us"--is an assumption that rests on our present inability to distinguish the elect from the reprobate. Grammatically, the phrase "Jesus Christ has endured death and suffering for them as well as for us" rests upon the "because" that precedes it: *"because" (pource que)* it is not ours to distinguish." The assertion of Christ's death for men in this general way is one that can only be made in light of ignorance. It is, by the same token, one that in Calvin's view must be made to prevent the stultification of the church's mission to the unbelieving.

The stance of the church toward the unbelieving world, in terms of prayer and preaching, mirrors closely the universal offer of the gospel. The church takes its marching orders from this source, not from the divine decree of election and reprobation.

In the final analysis, Calvin's doctrine of Christian activity toward the world was not unlike his doctrine of church discipline. In both cases, people need help. In both cases, there is an important working assumption which must be made for this help to be given: with the wayward brother, it is that because he is a member of the visible church he is a blood-bought soul; with the unbeliever outside the church, it is that Christ's death extends to him as well. In both cases, the assumption is based on a degree of ignorance about election and reprobation. And in both cases, the assumption creates an ethical imperative which to ignore is really to despise the blood of Christ and the souls for whom it was shed. So, in the end, Calvin extended a kind of "judgment of charity" even beyond the pale of the visible church. Only on the last day will the line of demarcation between the elect and the reprobate be as clear to human perception as it now is to God, and only then will God's treatment of human beings fully correspond to his decree.

[1] Sermon on Job 31:29-32, **CO** 34:696.

This is the proper framework for the interpretation of the last group of texts. There is no denial in them of the theological doctrine of limited redemption. There is, however, a firm caution against making the doctrine of limited redemption the basis of our action toward unbelievers.

13

CALVIN THE CALVINIST

The Amyraut thesis does not stand up under scrutiny. The individual statements which, when culled from Calvin's writings and quoted in lists, seem to speak of universal redemption, actually do not; the statements which seem to imply that some perish for whom Christ died are to be understood from the viewpoint of pastoral practice rather than from that of doctrinal assertion. In the end, Calvin turns out to be, on this point at least, a "Calvinist."

The question remains, however, why, if indeed Calvin was a limited redemptionist, it should require a lengthy treatise like this one to establish it. Calvin once said that the sum of his theology was contained in the **Institutes**. Then why does this doctrine of limited redemption not appear clearly in the **Institutes**? One topical treatment of the question of the extent of redemption there would have changed the course of subsequent historiography: Amyraut might still have developed his Reformed version of the Thomistic synthesis but would not have enlisted Calvin as a supporter, and several important works of modern scholarship would have taken a much different shape. The modern thesis regarding the rise of "Reformed scholasticism" might still have been formulated, but the contrast between Calvin and Beza could not have been so starkly put.

There are two explanations for the fact that limited redemption remained in Calvin's theology a doctrine in the background.

Why limited redemption remained in the background: history

The first is historical in nature. Calvin's antipredestinarian opponents never attacked him sharply or specifically enough on the matter of the extent of Christ's death to make him put the doctrine of limited redemption in the **Institutes**, at least in overt fashion. This is a strange thing. Calvin's adversaries made almost no use of the concept of universal redemption. In only two places was Calvin forced to answer objections to predestination based on universal redemption. Both of these occurred in **De aeterna dei praedestinatione**. The first is Calvin's response to Pighius's assertion that the proclamation of Christ as *redemptor mundi* militates against particular election;[1] the second was his answer to Georgius of Sicily's use of I John 2:2.[2] We have examined these texts. It must be admitted that these efforts of Pighius and Georgius were feeble indeed, and we wonder why they did not spend more time on this theme and bring to bear the large body of New Testament verses which teach Christ's death for "all" and for the "world." They seemed fixated on the more philosophical aspects of the contest--whether God is the author of sin, whether man has free will, whether man sins by necessity, and so forth. They seem not to have realized where their best weapons lay.

Pighius and Georgius were pamphlet foes; Calvin never dealt with them face to face. His flesh and blood foes, Jerome Bolsec and Sebastian Castellio, performed even more dismally when it came to opposing Calvin's doctrine of predestination. Bolsec's objections were recorded in detail by the authorities in Geneva throughout the fall of 1551;[3] among them there was no use whatsoever made of the concept of universal redemption or of the New Testament texts to that effect. Bolsec was absorbed by the philosophical implications of predestination and free will and very little concerned with the much more important soteriological and Christological implications.

Bolsec's case ended late in 1551. In 1558 Calvin was confronted by the objections of Sebastian Castellio. Bolsec may not have been completely out of the way; Beza believed that he was still agitating behind the scenes, and had a hand in the

---

[1] CO 8:298.

[2] CO 8:336.

[3] Cf. Philip E. Hughes, **The Register of the Company of Pastors of Geneva in the Time of Calvin** (Grand Rapids: Eerdmans Pub. Co., 1966), pp. 142-5, 163-5.

Castellio affair. Castellio's articles contained nothing on redemption. Like Bolsec, he centered on the questions of evil, morality, and contingency.[1] Once again, Calvin was not called upon to say anything about redemption. Why should he have brought up verses like I John 2:2, John 12:32, and I Tim. 2:6 when his opponents did not?

That Calvin's opponents seldom forced this issue does not mean, of course, that Calvin was unaware of it. He knew, as a student of theological history--the very theological history we traced in the first part of this study--and as a compatriot of Bucer's in Strassburg, that universal redemption had long been a staple of the antipredestinarian argument. His sensitivity to this surfaced most pointedly in the commentaries. And he sometimes proceeded as if in the face of imagined or anonymous objectors--"fanatics," he once called them--as if in a polemical situation.

Still, the question of the extent of redemption was not something which Calvin ever had to mobilize all his theological resources to address. For his own sake, it is hard to wish on him yet another controversy. But the modern scholar finds himself wishing that Calvin had been compelled, like Bucer, to deal with a persistent Bible-quoting Anabaptist like Melchior Hoffmann or a real theologian like Raban Maur, someone who would have insisted in no uncertain terms that Christ died for every human being and flung Bible verses at him to prove it. Faced with such a challenge, Calvin's position would have been publicly clarified, and the matter would certainly have found a place in the **Institutes**.

So the relative inaccessibility of Calvin's doctrine of limited redemption, the fact that it must be searched for in the commentaries, is in great measure due to the ineptitude of his theological adversaries. Later generations of Reformed theologians would face abler adversaries such as Arminius and Amyraut, who perceived the heart of the matter and who used the Bible as the Reformed did. These later Reformed theologians would be compelled to defend and define the doctrine of limited redemption

---

[1] Cf. Calvin's *ad seriatim* answer to Castellio's points in **De occulta Dei providentia, CO** 9:285-318.

in a more systematic way. As a result, the doctrine would make its way to the foreground of discussion and into the Reformed creeds. It was not, however, in this later setting, a new doctrine, but simply a newly embattled doctrine, not a departure from Calvin but the defense of what he had taught.

Thus the historical part of the answer. But all this does not explain why Calvin did not, of his own initiative, say something topically about limited redemption in the **Institutes**. At this point an explanation must be sought within the structure of his own theology, and in this connection two important points must be made.

Why limited redemption remained in the background: theology

The first is that limited redemption was always for Calvin part of a larger soteriological picture. This large picture was dominated by the Augustinian precept of the omnipotence of God and by ideas which were, in effect, corollaries of this precept: that what God wills to do he does, that the extent of God's saving will and work can be measured by the final outcome, and that the three persons of the Trinity act harmoniously and unitedly in the salvation of the predestined. There was also in Calvin--and here he improved considerably on Augustine--a well developed Christology in which the redemptive work of Christ was seen as an integrated unity. As has been demonstrated, these large soteriological themes assumed and necessitated that the death of Christ be particular in its intention. There was no need for Calvin to demonstrate separately, as if the matter were a *locus theologicus* in its own right, that Christ did not die for the reprobate. The idea of universal redemption would have instantly created massive jagged tears in the fabric of Calvin's gospel: the divine will would have been severed from its effectuation, the work of the Son from that of the Father and the Spirit, and the death of the Mediator from his resurrection, intercession, and rule. It would also have made the role which Calvin assigned to Christ in election inexplicable.

For all these reasons, there could be no such thing in Calvin's theology as Christ dying for someone and that person not being finally saved. The statements about people perishing for whom

Christ died were, as we have argued, no exception to this rule. If it were possible for the death of Christ, as the saving act of the omnipotent God through his divine Son, to prove unfruitful, than the divine will would be undercut, man thrown back into radical contingency, and the assurance of salvation, to the extent that it is rooted in Christ, destroyed.

There was something else in Calvin's theology which explains the relative inconspicuousness of his doctrine of limited redemption. Calvin did indeed deny that Christ died for the reprobate. But Calvin did not regard the denial of Christ's death for the reprobate as a part of the gospel proclamation *per se*. The gospel was not that Christ did *not* die for certain people; the gospel for Calvin was the astounding good news that Christ *did* die for people, and it was this theme which he so evidently delighted in expounding. This was the doctrine in the foreground. Nor did Calvin normally perceive the powerful universalistic emphasis of the New Testament as a threat. He embraced it. The kingdom of God, Calvin believed, had spilled over the confining barriers of Judaism to the nations, and Jesus was now the universal Messiah, the Savior of all, and was to be proclaimed as the only source of reconciliation. He was for Calvin the Redeemer of the world.

Christ, redeemer of the church, redeemer of the world

This enthusiastic universalism did not bring with it for Calvin the doctrine that Christ by his death redeemed all individuals. We have been critical of Amyraut, but perhaps Amyraut should not be faulted too much for not perceiving this. Perhaps the seventeenth century defenders of limited redemption had lost the spirit, the feeling, of Calvin's universalism in their theology, so much so that it was difficult for Amyraut to imagine that someone could in fact hold and believe in limited redemption while proclaiming Christ as *redemptor mundi*. In Calvin's theology there coexisted both an uncompromising Augustinian particularism and the proclamation of Christ as Redeemer of the world.

It was a difficult balance to preserve. One emphasis tended to swallow the other up. The Reformed orthodoxy of the seventeenth century tended to let Calvin's universalism be eclipsed; Amyraut, overreacting in the other direction, seriously compromised Calvin's particularism. And the assumption is also common with modern scholars that the doctrine of limited redemption and the proclamation of the death of Christ for the world are mutually exclusive. So, argues much of the modern scholarship, Reformed orthodoxy after Calvin, if it lost Calvin's universalism, must have done so because of the introduction of limited redemption; by the same logic, if Calvin himself was a preacher of Christ as *redemptor mundi* then he cannot possibly have been a limited redemptionist. It is ironic that the historians who criticize Reformed orthodoxy in this way do so because they share precisely the same logical axiom which they impute to it: that Christ as *redemptor ecclesiae* and Christ as *redemptor mundi* cannot coexist in one system.

Calvin's soteriology preserved both the doctrine of limited redemption and the full-blooded proclamation of the cross of Christ to every human being. Whether this integration was valid on the biblical *criteria* against which Calvin himself desired to be judged is an assessment which we have not attempted to make. The point of this study is an historical one: it simply cannot be maintained, as an *historical* judgment, that limited redemption ruins a theology from the inside and undermines assurance and gospel preaching. Augustine, Bucer, Calvin--all of them had grand conceptions of the universality of the work of Christ. And Gottschalk, perhaps the most "infamous" limited redemptionist of all, was missionizing the pagan Bulgars while his future opponents sat in the relative comfort of Christian France. This must be allowed to inform the kinds of conclusions which historians make about the course of Reformed theology after Calvin. Whatever changes may have occurred, they cannot be traced to the alleged introduction of limited redemption by Beza. Limited redemption was the doctrine of Calvin, and had been deep in the bloodstream of predestinarian theology for more than a thousand years.

14

REFORMED THEOLOGY IN PERSPECTIVE

In the light of what we have seen, both of the history of strict Augustinianism before Calvin and of Calvin's theology itself, Reformed theology (or "Calvinism") comes into focus as part of a larger story.

Reasserting Augustine

In the long view, the Reformation, and especially Reformed theology, should be seen as part of a long line of "Augustinian outbreaks." The millennium following Augustine was punctuated by efforts to revive and reassert his mature predestinarianism in its fullest sense--and that includes the doctrine of limited redemption. Of these efforts, the Gottschalk movement of the ninth century and the critique of the church offered by Wyclif and Hus in the 14th-15th centuries were the most disruptive. Nor was Reformed theology the last of these outbreaks, for the Jansenist movement of the seventeenth century would belong to the same historical tradition. But Reformed theology was undoubtedly the most successful.

Before the Reformation, the Augustinian outbreaks had been either squelched or successfully weathered by the Catholic church, and the doctrine of limited redemption had remained, at best, on the fringe. Sometimes it had been considered heresy. It certainly never became what its defenders wanted it to become, the dominant and official theology of the Catholic church. But this long "exile" was to end in the sixteenth century. It is true that in Lutheranism, in spite of the Augustinianism of Luther himself, the familiar process of modification and synthesis took place, so that by the late sixteenth century Lutheran theology vigorously affirmed universal redemption and condemned limited redemption. In the Reformed tradition, however, the doctrine of limited redemption became, for the first time, the stated and official orthodoxy of a considerable body of Christians with international representation. The Canons of Dort (1619) and the Westminster Confession of Faith (1647) represented the culmination of this development. In the Reformed churches, Augustine's whole particularism, long a kind of theological black sheep, finally found an ecclesiastical home.

Leaving Augustine behind, quietly

But as soon as we affirm the continuity of Reformed theology with the Augustinian tradition, we must add that the old bishop of Hippo would not have been entirely happy. For the victory of his soteriology in Reformed theology was achieved at the expense of his teaching about the church and the sacraments. Here the Roman Catholic church had a better claim to Augustine's sponsorship than the reformers did. Augustine the anti-Pelagian (the Augustine whom the reformers chiefly followed) saw salvation as the sovereign and secret work of God in predestined individuals; Augustine the anti-Donatist spoke of salvation as a work of God mediated through the institution of the church, and particularly through its sacraments. Perhaps Augustine himself had these things reconciled at some rarified level in his own mind, but his successors found the two strands hard to keep together. Hincmar squeezed Gottschalk between the objectivity of redemption (Augustine's soteriology) and the objectivity of baptism (Augustine's sacramental doctrine), and Gottschalk squirmed. The predestinarianism of Wyclif and Hus was rightly perceived by the churchmen of their day as a dire threat to the very "institutionalality" of the church. These were symptoms of the tension Augustine had bequeathed to Catholic theology. Yet it was left to the Reformation, and to Reformed theology in particular, to opt decisively for the anti-Pelagian over the anti-Donatist Augustine. In Reformed theology the role of church and sacrament as means of grace was consistently subordinated to the sovereign work of God in the hearts of the elect. The church, to be sure, retained an institutional character--the Reformed were no spiritualists--but there was still undeniably a shift away from the ecclesiology which had dominated Catholicism since Augustine.

The Reformed saw the church as the *milieu* in which the preaching of the word and the reception of the sacraments takes place, but they did not bind the grace of God to these means. The efficacy of the church's ministry depends on the election of God. The sacramental objection used against Gottschalk would not have bothered the Reformed, because the Reformed did not see baptism or the Lord's Supper as objective grace.

This thesis may run into the objection that the magisterial reformers hung doggedly on to the anti-Donatist Augustine as well. So they did, but here we question whether they had a theological right to do so. The Roman Catholic claim to have this Augustine on its side stung the reformers, precisely because it had substance. The reformers wanted to be considered "catholic"; they claimed not to be revolutionaries but restorers of the true catholic church; but the fact was that they had broken from the institution of the Catholic church. They must have realized deep in their hearts that this was essentially a Donatistic thing they had done. So it was immensely convenient to have various kinds of Anabaptists around at whom to fling the epithet "Donatist," and the reformers did so with much zeal to prove their catholicity. In spite of all this effort, it seems difficult to harmonize the actions of the reformers with an Augustinian ecclesiology, and the judgment of B. B. Warfield must stand, even over the objections that the reformers would doubtless make against it: "The Reformation, inwardly considered, was just the ultimate triumph of Augustine's doctrine of grace over Augustine's doctrine of the church."[1] Had Augustine been suddenly transplanted to the sixteenth century, would he have joined the Catholics or the Protestants?

Refashioning Augustine

Reformed theology, for all its faithfulness to Augustine's

---

[1] B. B. Warfield, **Calvin and Augustine** (Philadelphia: Presbyterian and Reformed, 1956), p. 322. Pelikan says of this well-known quotation that it is an exaggeration but not a distortion. (Pelikan, 4:9) He also sees in Augustine two strands which were not finally "unravelled until the Reformation." 4:19.

theology of grace, did something else that was new: it took Augustine's particularism and placed it under the control of a new motive power: forensic justification and assurance. As an *Augustinian* theology, Reformed theology repeated old themes; as a *Reformation* theology, it proclaimed as the centerpoint of the gospel the doctrine of justification by faith alone. Calvin, for one, was candid enough to admit that at this crucial point his own theology diverged from Augustine's, who, for all his keen insight into the monergism of grace, had taught an infused righteousness rather than an imputed.[1] So there was a parting of the ways here, and a new alignment of doctrines. Particularism came together with *justificatio sola fide* and, as a result of this fusion, the doctrines of predestination and limited redemption were harnessed in the service of Christian assurance. This was a major transformation. For the medieval predestinarians, as well as for the theology of the Counter-Reformation Catholic church,[2] the kind of militant assurance which the reformers taught was presumptuous, even sacriligious; it was impossible apart from special revelation. Wyclif, for example, for all his confidence in the omnipotence of God, had no real doctrine of assurance; he counseled a kind of quiet and accepting hopefulness in the mercy of God and the faithful use of the means of grace. There was no way for the Christian to tap into the omnipotence of God as a source of comfort and security. This was not acceptable in any truly Reformation theology. The Reformation was born in the crisis of assurance and its deepest motive was to provide the believer with that unassailable assurance without which Christian life and service would, in the estimation of the reformers, be crippled. So, in the hands of Calvin, predestination and redemption became radically Christocentric themes, doctrines of the heart, fighting doctrines; by faith in Christ the believer can and must know his own election and can get on with serving God. This new use of the predestinarian complex of ideas cannot be

---

[1] Inst. 3.11.15.

[2] Cf. the pronouncement of Trent on assurance, in **Concilium Tridentinum: Diariorum, Actorum, Epistolarum, Tractatium nova Collectio**, 10 vols. (Freiburg, 1901-), 5:393.

overstressed as a great discontinuity between the Augustinianism of the later middle ages and that of Reformed theology.

Who was the real "scholastic"?

Finally, looking forward from Calvin, a word on Amyraut and Reformed orthodoxy. It is one of the commonplaces of the prevailing scholarly viewpoint that Reformed orthodoxy, and the doctrine of limited redemption in particular, was "scholastic." Perhaps this historical construction should be modified in light of the fact that it was Amyraut's theology, not Beza's, that most closely reflected the Thomistic synthesis. This resemblance was probably not accidental. Amyraut's mentor, John Cameron, had connected the Reformed covenant idea to the "antecedent" and "consequent" loves of God; the language of Thomas was clearly recognizable in this. Both Thomas and Amyraut were genuine predestinarians; both of them also believed in universal redemption. The genius of Amyraut, and of Cameron before him, was to restate Thomas' synthesis of particularism and universalism in the covenantal terminology more congenial to Reformed theology. Of course, "scholastic" is not a word with a theological content; it simply refers to the theology done in the medieval schools, or universities. But inasmuch as some modern historians have filled it with a certain (unquestionably negative) content, applying it to Reformed orthodoxy in order to distance it from Calvin, or to argue that Calvin and Amyraut represented a "humanistic" kind of Reformed theology as opposed to "Reformed scholasticism," we are justified in challenging the label. In fact, it seems much more accurate to say that Amyraut was the real Reformed "scholastic," the Reformed "Thomas Aquinas," the balancer, the synthesizer, the creator of new categories and structures. And Reformed orthodoxy, with its insistence on limited redemption, was actually a primitive throwback to the rigorous and markedly non-rationalistic particularism of Augustine and Gottschalk.

Under whatever label, John Calvin, as a limited redemptionist, belongs historically with Augustine, Gottschalk, Bucer, Beza, and Reformed orthodoxy--not with Amyraut.

SELECTED BIBLIOGRAPHY

Original Sources

Acta Synodi Dordrechti. Dort, 1620.

Amyraut, Moyse. Brief Traitté de la predestination et de ses principales dependances. Saumur: J. Lesnier, 1634.

_____. Brief Traité de la Predestination. Avec l'Eschantillon de la doctrine de Calvin sur le mesme suiet. Saumur: Desbordes, 1658.

_____. Defense de la doctrine de Calvin sur le sujet de l'election et de la reprobation. Saumur: Desbordes, 1644.

_____. Dissertationes theologicae sex. Quarum quator De oeconomia trium personarum, De jure Dei in creaturas, De gratia universali, De gratia particulari, antehac editae, nunc revisae prodeunt; DUAE, De serpente tentatore, Et de peccato originis, ad superiores additae sunt. Saumur: Desbordes, 1660.

_____. Fidei Mosis Amyraldi circa errores Arminianorum declaratio. Saumur: Lesnier, 1646.

_____. Sermons sur divers textes de la sainte ecriture. 2nd edition. Saumur: Desbordes, 1653.

Anselm, St. Anselm of Canterbury, Vol. 3. Translated and edited by Jasper Hopkins and Herbert Richardson. Toronto and New York: The Edwin Mellen Press, 1976.

Beze, Theodore de. De praedestinationis doctrina et vero usu tractatio absolutissima. Ex Th. Bezae praelectionibus in nonum Epistolae ad Romanos caput a Raphaele Eglino Tigurino Theologiae studioso in schola Genevensi recens excepta. Genevae, 1582.

_____. Volumen primum (-tertium) Tractationum Theologicarum, in quibus pleraque Christianae Religionis dogmata adversus haereses nostris temporibus renovatas solide ex Verbo Dei defenduntur, Editio secunda ad ipso Auctore recognita. Genevae, 1582.

Bucer, Martin. **Martin Bucers Deutsche Schriften.** 8 vols. Edited by Robert Stupperich. Gütersloh: Gerd Mohn, 1960-.

_____. **In sacra quator evangelia, Enarrationes perpetuae, secundum recognitae, in quibus praeterea habes syncerioris Theologiae locos communes supra centum ad scripturarum fidem simpliciter, & nullius cum insectatione tractatos, adiectis etiam aliquot locorum retractationibus.** Basileae: Iohannes Hervagius, 1536.

_____. **Metaphrases et enarrationes perpetuae epistolarum D. Pauli Apostoli... Tomus primus. Continens metaphrasim et enarrationem in Epistolam ad Romanos.** Argentorati: VVendelinus Rihelius, 1536.

_____. **Praelectiones doctiss. in epistolam D. P. ad Ephesios, eximij doctoris D. Martini Buceri...** Basileae: Petrus Perna, 1562.

_____. **Tomus Anglicanus.** 1577.

Calvin, John. **Calvin's Calvinism.** Translated and edited by H. Cole. Grand Rapids: Wm. B. Eerdmans Pub. Co., 1956.

_____. **Concerning the Eternal Predestination of God.** Translated by J. K. S. Reid. London: Clarke, 1961.

_____. **Corpus Reformatorum. Ioannis Calvini opera quae supersunt omnia.** 59 vols. Edited by G. Baum, E. Cunitz, and E. Reuss. Brunswick and Berlin: Schwetschke, 1863-1900.

_____. **Institutes of the Christian Religion.** Edited by John McNeill. Library of Christian Classics XX, XXI. Philadelphia: Westminster Press, 1961.

_____. **Johannis Calvini Opera Selecta.** 5 vols. Edited by P. Barth and W. Niesel. Muenchen: D. Scheuner, 1926-52.

_____. **Sermons on Ephesians.** Edinburgh: Banner of Truth, 1973.

_____. **Sermons on Galatians.** Translated by Arthur Golding. London: Bynneman, 1574.

_____. **Sermons on Isaiah's Prophecy of the Death and Passion of Christ.**

188

Translated and edited by T. H. L. Parker. London: James Clarke & Co., 1956.

_____. Sermons on Job. Translated by Arthur Golding. London, 1580.

_____. Sermons on the Fifth Book of Moses Called Deuteronomy. Translated by Arthur Golding. London, 1583.

Supplementa Calviniana. Sermons inedits. Neukirchen, 1961-.

_____. The Deity of Christ and Other Sermons. Translated by Leroy Nixon. Grand Rapids: Wm. B. Eerdmans Pub. Co., 1950.

_____. The Mystery of Godliness and other selected sermons. Grand Rapids: Wm. B. Eerdmans Pub. Co., 1950.

_____. The Theological Treatises. Translated by J. K. S. Reid. Library of Christian Classics XXII. Philadelphia: Westminster Press, 1960.

_____. Thirteen Sermons of Maister John Calvine, Entreating of the Free Election of God in Jacob, and of Reprobation in Esau. London, 1579.

Capito, Wolfgang. Preface to De Operibus Dei Martin Cellario authore. Argentorati, 1527.

Concilium Tridentinum: Diariorum, Actorum, Epistolarum, Tractatiuum nova Collectio. 12 vols. Freiburg, 1901-.

Corpus Christianorum, Series Latina. Turnholti: Typographi Brepols Editores Pontificii, 1953-.

Denck, Hans. Schriften. 2. Teil. Religiöse Schriften. Edited by Walter Fellmann. Quellen und Forschungen zur Reformationsgeschichte XXIV. Quellen zur Geschichte der Täufer VI. Gütersloh: C. Bertelsmann Verlag, 1956.

Du Moulin, Pierre. De Mosis Amyraldi adversus Fridericum Spanheimium libro judicium. Rotterdam, 1649.

_____. Esclaircissement des controverses salmuriennes ou Defense de la doctrine des Eglises reformees. Leyde, 1648.

_____. Examen de la doctrine de MM. Amyrault & Testard. Amsterdam,

1638.

Gottschalk. **Oeuvres théologiques et grammaticales de Godescalc d'Orbais.** Edited by Cyrille Lambot. Louvain, 1945.

Gregory of Rimini. **Gregorii Ariminensis Oesa Lectura Super Primum et Secundum Sententiarum. Tomus III.** Edited by A. Damasus Trapp osa and Venecio Marcolino. Spätmittelalter und Reformation Texte und Untersuchung. Edited by Heiko Oberman. Berlin, New York: Walter de Gruyter, 1984.

Hus, John. **John Hus, The Church.** Translated by David S. Schaff. New York: Charles Scribners Sons, 1915.

_____. **Magister Joannis Hus, Super IV. Sententiarum.** Edited by W. Flajshans and M. Kominkova. Osnabrück: Biblio-Verlag, 1966.

_____. **Magistri Johannis Hus, Sermones de tempori qui Collecta dicuntur.** Edited by Anezka Schmidtova. Praha: Academia scientiarum Bohemoslovanica, 1959.

_____. **Magistri Johannis Hus Tractatus de Ecclesia.** Edited by S. Harrison Thomson. Boulder, Colo.: University of Colorado Press, 1956.

Luther, Martin. **Lectures on Romans.** Translated and edited by Wilhelm Pauck. Library of Christian Classics XV. London: SCM Press, 1961.

_____. **Luther's Works.** 54 vols. Saint Louis: Concordia Publishing House. 1958-67.

Monumenta Germaniae Historica. Berlin, 1826-.

Patrologia Cursus Completus, Series Graeca. Edited by J. P. Migne. Paris, 1857-66.

Patrologia Cursus Completus, Series Latina. Edited by J. P. Migne. Paris, 1878-90.

Quellen zur Geschichte der Täufer. 14 vols. Gütersloh: Gerd Mohn, 1930-. Vol 7: **Elsass, I. Teil, Stadt Strassburg 1522-32.** Edited by Manfred Krebs and Hans Georg Rott, 1959. Vol. 8: **Elsass, I. Teil, Stadt Strassburg 1532-34.** Edited by Manfred Krebs and Hans Georg Rott, 1960.

The Register of the Company of Pastors of Geneva in the time of Calvin. Edited by Philip E. Hughes. Grand Rapids: Wm. B. Eerdmans, 1966.

Rivet, André. Andreae Riveti...synopsis doctrinae natura et gratia. Excerpta ex Mosis Amyraldi...tractatu de praedestinatione... Amsterdam, 1649.

Rothmann, Bernhard. Die Schriften Bernhard Rothmanns. Edited by Robert Stupperich. Die Schriften der münsterischen Täufer und ihrer Gegner, 1. Teil. Muenster in Westfalen: Aschendorffsche Verlagsbuchhandlung, 1970.

Spanheim, Frederick. Disputatio de gratia universali. Leyden, 1644.

_____. Exercitationes de gratia universali... Leyden, 1644.

_____. Vindiciarum pro exercitationibus suis de gratia universali...adversus Amyraldi. Amsterdam, 1649.

Spiritual and Anabaptist Writers. Edited by George H. Williams. Philadelphia: Westminster Press, 1957.

Staupitz, Johannes von. Libellus de executione Eterne Predestinationis. Nuremberg, 1517.

Thomas Aquinas. Summa Theologica. Romae: Ex Typographia Forzani et S., 1894.

_____. Super Epistolas S. Pauli Lectura. Romae: Marietti, 1953.

Ursinus, Zacharias. Explicationem Catecheticarum D. Zachariae Ursini Silesii. Neostadii Palatinorum: Matthei Harnisch, 1595.

Wyclif, John. Wyclif's Latin Works. 34 vols. London: The Wyclif Society, 1883-1914.

Secondary Sources

Anderson, James Wm. *The Grace of God and the Non-elect in Calvin's Commentaries and Sermons.* Th.D. dissertation, New Orleans Baptist Seminary, 1976.

Anrich, Gustave. **Martin Bucer.** Strasbourg, 1914.

Armstrong, Brian. **Calvinism and the Amyraut Heresy: Protestant Scholasticism and Humanism in Seventeenth Century France.** Madison: The University of Wisconsin Press, 1969.

Bangs, Carl. **Arminius. A Study in the Dutch Reformation.** Nashville, New York: Abingdon Press, 1971.

Bavaud, G. *La doctrine de la predéstination et de la reprobation d'après s. Augustin et Calvin.* **Revue des etudes augustiniennes** 5 (1959):431-38.

Beechy, Alvin J. **The Concept of Grace in the Radical Reformation.** Bibl. Humanistica et Reformatorica 17. Nieuwkoop: De Graaf, 1977.

Bell, M. Charles. *Calvin and the Extent of the Atonement.* **Evangelical Quarterly** 55 (April 1983):115-23.

_____. *Was Calvin a Calvinist?* **Scottish Journal of Theology** 36, No. 4 (1983):535-40.

Bizer, Ernst. **Frühorthodoxie und Rationalismus.** Zurich, 1963.

Bornkamm, Heinrich. **Martin Bucers Bedeutung für de Europäische Reformationsgeschichte.** Gütersloh, 1952.

Bray, John S. **Theodore Beza's Doctrine of Predestination.** Nieuwkoop: De Graaf, 1975.

Brown, Peter. **Augustine of Hippo. A Biography.** London: Faber & Faber, 1967.

Brunner, Emil. **The Mediator.** Philadelphia: Westminster Press, 1947.

Choisy, Eugene. *Grace in the Theology of the Reformers: Calvin.* In **The Doctrine of Grace.** Edited by W. T. Whitley. London: Student Christian

Movement Press, 1932.

Clarke, F. Stuart. *Arminius's Understanding of Calvin*. Evangelical Quarterly 54 (Jan.-March 1982):25-35.

Collins, Ross Wm. **Calvin and the Libertines of Geneva.** Toronto, Vancouver: Clarke, Irwin & Co. Ltd., 1968.

Courvoisier, Jacques. *Bucer et Calvin.* In **Calvin à Strasbourg 1538 bis 1541. Quatre études,** pp. 37-66. Strasbourg, 1938.

Dantine, J. *Die Prädestinationslehre bei Calvin und Beza.* Ph.D. dissertation, Göttingen, 1965.

Davis, Kenneth R. **Anabaptism and Asceticism. A Study in Intellectual Origins.** Scottdale, Pa.: Herald Press, 1974.

De Klerk, Peter. *Calvin Bibliography.* **Calvin Theological Journal** 12- (1977-). [This is a yearly bibliographical update on Calvin studies.]

De Kroon, Marijn and Krueger, Friedhelm (eds.). **Bucer und seine Zeit.** Wiesbaden: Franz Steiner Verlag, 1976.

Doumergue, Emile. **Jean Calvin: les hommes et les choses de son temps.** 8 vols. Geneve: Slatkin Reprints, 1969.

Dowey, E. A. **The Knowledge of God in Calvin's Theology.** New York, 1952.

Eells, Hastings. **Martin Bucer.** New Haven, 1931.

Engelland, Heinrich. **Gott und Mensch bei Calvin.** Munich: Kaiser, 1934.

Erichson, Alfredus. **Bibliographia Calviniana.** Nieuwdoop: De Graaf, 1960.

Foley, George. **Anselm's Theory of the Atonement.** New York: Longman's, Green, and Co., 1909.

Franks, Robert S. **The Work of Christ.** London and New York, 1962.

Ganoczy, Alexander and Scheld, Stefan. **Die Hermeneutik Calvins.** Veröffentlichungen des Instituts für Europäische Geschichte Mainz. Wiesbaden: Franz Steiner Verlag, 1983.

Godfrey, W. Robert. *Reformed Thought on the Extent of the Atonement to 1618.* Westminster Theological Journal 37 (Winter 1975).

_____. *Tensions within International Calvinism: The Debate on the Atonement at the Synod of Dort 1618-19.* Ph.D. dissertation, Stanford University, 1974.

Goertz, Hans-Jürgen. **Profiles of Radical Reformers.** Translated by Walter Klaassen. Goshen, Ind.: Herald Press, 1982.

Goeters, J. F. Gerhard. **Ludwig Hätzer, Spiritualist und Antitrinitarier.** Quellen und Forschungen zur Reformationsgeschichte, Band XXV. Gütersloh: C. Bertelsmann Verlag, 1957.

Goumaz, Louis. **La doctrine de salut (doctrina salutis) d'après le commentaires de Calvin sur le Nouveau Testament.** Lyon, 1917.

Gründler, Otto. **Die Gotteslehre Giralmo Zanchis.** Beiträge zur Geschichte und Lehre der Reformierten Kirche, Vol. 20. Neukirchen, 1965.

_____. *Thomism and Calvinism in the Theology of Girolami Zanchi.* Th.D. dissertation, Princeton Theological Seminary, 1963.

Hall, Basil. *Calvin against the Calvinists.* In **John Calvin: A Collection of Distinguished Essays.** Edited by Gervase E. Duffield. Grand Rapids, 1966.

_____. *From Biblical Humanism to Calvinist Orthodoxy.* **Journal of Ecclesiastical History** 31 (1980):335-36, 339-40.

Hauck, Albert. **Kirchengeschichte Deutschlands.** 5 vols. Berlin: Akademie-Verlag, 1903-20.

Hauck, Wilhelm-Albert. **Die Erwählten: Pradestination und Heilsgewissheit nach Calvin.** Gütersloh: C. Bertelsmann Verlag, 1950.

Hefele, Carl Joseph. **Histoire des Conciles d'après les documents originaux.** 11 vols. Translated by Henri Leclercq. Paris: Letouzey et Ané, editeurs. 1907-52.

Helm, Paul. **Calvin and the Calvinists.** Edinburgh: Banner of Truth, 1982.

_____. *Calvin, English Calvinism and the Logic of Doctrinal Development.*

Scottish Journal of Theology 34, No. 2 (1981):179-85.

Jacobs, Paul. **Prädestination und Verantwortlichkeit bei Calvin.** Neukirchen, 1937.

Jansen, John Frederick. **Calvin's Doctrine of the Work of Christ.** London: J. Clarke, 1956.

Janz, Denis R. **Luther and Late Medieval Thomism: A Study in Theological Anthropology.** Waterloo: Wilfrid Laurier University Press, 1983.

Kawerau, Peter. **Melchior Hoffmann als Religiöser Dencker.** Haarlem: De Erven F. Bohn N. V., 1954.

Kempff, D. **A Bibliography of Calviniana 1959-1974.** Studies in Medieval and Reformation Thought, Vol. XV. Leiden: E. J. Brill, 1975.

Kendall, R. T. **Calvin and English Calvinism to 1649.** Oxford: The University Press, 1979.

Kickel, Walter. **Vernunft und Offenbarung bei Theodor Beza.** Beiträge zur Geschichte und Lehre der Reformierten Kirche, Vol. 25. Neukirchen, 1967.

Kittelson, James M. **Wolfgang Capito: From Humanist to Reformer.** Leiden: Brill, 1975.

Klaassen, Walter. **Anabaptism, Neither Catholic nor Protestant.** Waterloo, Ontario: Conrad Press, 1973.

Klooster, Fred. **Calvin's Doctrine of Predestination.** Grand Rapids, 1961.

Krahn, Henry. *An Analysis of the Conflict between the Clergy of the Reformed Church and the Leaders of the Anabaptist Movement in Strasbourg, 1524-34.* Ph.D. dissertation, University of Washington, 1969.

Lang, August. **Der Evangelienkommentar Martin Bucers und die Grundzüge seiner Theologie.** Leipzig, 1900.

_____. *Martin Bucer.* Evangelical Quarterly 1 (April 1929).

Laplanche, François. **Orthodoxie et Prédication: L'Oeuvre d'Amyraut et la querelle de la grâce universelle.** Paris, 1965.

Leff, Gordon. Bradwardine and the Pelagians: A Study of his "De Causa Dei" and its Opponents. Cambridge, 1957.

_____. Gregory of Rimini: Tradition and Innovation in Fourteenth Century Thought. Manchester, 1961.

Letham, R. W. A. *Saving Faith and Assurance in Reformed Theology: Zwingli to the Synod of Dort.* Ph.D. dissertation, Aberdeen, 1979.

Lexikon für Theologie und Kirche. 11 vols. Freiburg: Verlag Herder, 1957-67.

Lightner, Robert. The Death Christ Died: A Case for Unlimited Atonement. Des Plaines, Ill.: Regular Baptist, 1967.

Loserth, Johann. Huss und Wiclif. München und Berlin: R. Oldenbourg, 1925.

McGrath, A. E. *'Augustinianism'? A Critical Assessment of the So-called 'Medieval Augustinian Tradition' on Justification.* Augustiniana 31 (1981).

McPhee, Ian. *Conserver of Transformer of Calvin's Thought? A Study of the Origins and Development of Theodore Beza's Thought 1550-70.* Ph.D. dissertation, Cambridge, 1979.

Milner, Benjamin Charles, Jr. Calvin's Doctrine of the Church. Leiden: E. J. Brill, 1970.

Mitchell, Charles Buell. *Martin Bucer and Sectarian Dissent: A Confrontation of the Magisterial Reformation with Anabaptists and Spiritualists.* Ph.D. dissertation, Yale, 1960.

Moltmann, Juergen. *Gnadenbund und Gnadenwahl: Die Prädestinationslehre des Moyse Amyrault, dargestellt im Zusammenhang der heilgeschichtlich-foederaltheologie Tradition der Akademie von Saumur.* Ph.D. dissertation, Göttingen, 1951.

Mozley, J. B. A Treatise on the Augustinian Doctrine of Predestination. London, 1855.

Muller, Richard A. Christ and the Decree: Christology and Predestination in Reformed Theology from Calvin to Perkins. Grand Rapids: Baker Book House, 1988.

196

Murray, John. *Calvin on the Extent of the Atonement.* Banner of Truth 234 (March 1983):20-22.

Nicole, Roger. **Moyse Amyraut. A Bibliography. With Special Reference to the Controversy on Universal Grace.** New York, London: Garland Pub. Co., 1981.

Niesel, Wilhelm. **Calvin-Bibliographie 1901-1959.** Muenchen: Chr. Kaiser Verlag, 1961.

_____. **The Theology of Calvin.** Translated by Harold Knight. Philadelphia: Westminster Press, 1956.

Oberman, Heiko. **Archbishop Thomas Bradwardine, a Fourteenth-century Augustinian.** Utrecht: Kemink, 1958.

_____. **Forerunners of the Reformation.** New York: Holt, Rinehart, & Winston, 1966.

Otten, Hans. **Calvins theologische Anschauung von der Prädestination.** Munich, 1938.

Parker, T. H. L. **Calvin's New Testament Commentaries.** London: SCM Press, Ltd., 1971.

_____. **John Calvin: A Biography.** London: J. M. Dent & Sons, Ltd., 1975.

_____. **The Oracles of God: An Introduction to the Preaching of John Calvin.** London: Lutterworth Press, 1947.

Pauck, Wilhelm. *Calvin and Butzer.* Journal of Religion 9 (1929):237-56.

Pelikan, Jaroslav. **The Christian Tradition: A History of the Development of Doctrine.** 4 vols. Chicago: University of Chicago Press, 1971-.

Peterson, Robert A. **Calvin's Doctrine of the Atonement.** Phillipsburg, N. J.: Presbyterian and Reformed Pub. Co., 1983.

Pollet, J. V. **Martin Bucer: études sur la correspondance.** 2 vols. Paris, 1958, 1962.

Reid, J. K. S. *The Office of Christ in Predestination.* Scottish Journal of

Theology 1 (1948):5-19, 166-83.

Schaefer, Harry. *The Doctrine of Atonement in the Writings of Luther and Calvin*. Ph.D. dissertation, University of Chicago, 1920.

Schaff, Philip. **History of the Christian Church**. 8 vols. Grand Rapids: Wm. B. Eerdmans Pub. Co., 1950.

Scheibe, Max. **Calvins Prädestinationslehre**. Halle: Druck von Ehrhardt Karras, 1897.

Schweizer, Alexander. **Die Protestantischen Centraldogmen in ihrer Entwicklung innerhalb der Reformierten Kirche**. 2 vols. Zurich, 1854-56.

Selinger, Suzanne. **Calvin against Himself. An Inquiry in Intellectual History**. Hamden, Conn.: Archon Books, 1984.

Sharp, Larry. *The Doctrine of Grace in Calvin and Augustine*. **Evangelical Quarterly** 52 (April-June 1980):84-96.

Smits, Luchesius. **Saint Augustin dans l'oeuvre de Jean Calvin**. Assen: Van Gorcum & Comp. N. V. -- G. A. Hak & Dr. H. J. Prakke, 1957.

Spinka, Matthew. **John Hus. A Biography**. Princeton, N. J.: Princeton University Press, 1968.

_____. **John Hus' Concept of the Church**. Princeton, N. J.: Princeton University Press, 1966.

Steinmetz, David C. **Reformers in the Wings**. Philadelphia, 1971.

Stickelberger, Emanuel. **Calvin: A Life**. Translated by D. G. Gelzer. Richmond, Va.: John Knox Press, 1961.

Stephens, W. P. **The Holy Spirit in the Theology of Martin Bucer**. Cambridge, 1970.

Thompson, Bard. *Bucer Study since 1918*. **Church History** 25, 1 (1956):63-82.

Turmel, J. *Histoire de l'interprétation de 1. Tim. 2,4*. **Revue d'histoire et litter. rel.** 5 (1900):385-415.

Tylenda, J. N. *Calvin Bibliography 1960-70.* Calvin Theological Journal 6, No. 2. [more]

Van Buren, Paul. **Christ in our Place: The Substitutionary Character of Calvin's Doctrine of Reconciliation.** Edinburgh: Oliver and Boyd, 1957.

Vander Scharf, Mark E. *Predestination and Certainty of Salvation in Augustine and Calvin.* Reformed Review 1 (1979):63-71.

Vielhaber, Claus. **Gottschalk der Sachse.** Bonn, 1956.

Vignaux, Paul. **Justification et Prédestination au XIVe Siecle.** Paris: Libraire Ernest Leroux, 1934.

Wallace, Dewey. **Puritans and Predestination.** Chapel Hill: University of North Carolina Press, 1982.

_____. *The Doctrine of Predestination in the Early English Reformation.* **Church History** 43 (1974):201-15.

Warfield, B. B. **Calvin and Augustine.** Philadelphia: Presbyterian and Reformed Publishing Co., 1956.

Wells, David. *Decretum Dei Speciale. An Analysis of the Content and Significance of Calvin's Doctrine of Soteriological Predestination.* Th.M. thesis, Trinity Evangelical Divinity School, 1967.

Wendel, François. **Calvin et l'Humanisme.** Cahiers de la revue d'histoire et de philosophie religieuses 45. Paris: Presses Universitaires de France, 1976.

_____. **John Calvin: The Origins and Development of his Religious Thought.** Translated by Philip Mairet. London: Wm. Collins and Sons, 1963.

_____. **Martin Bucer.** Strasbourg, 1952.

Wiley, David N. *Calvin's Doctrine of Predestination: His Principal Soteriological and Polemical Doctrine.* Ph.D. dissertation, Duke University, 1971.

Williams, George H. **The Radical Reformation.** Philadelphia: The Westminster Press, 1962.

INDEX OF BIBLE PASSAGES

INDEX OF NAMES